# It's Easy To
# Music Theory

### by Joe Bennett

**Wise Publications**
London/New York/Paris/Sydney/Copenhagen/Madrid/Tokyo

Exclusive Distributors:
Music Sales Limited
8/9 Frith Street, London W1D 3JB, England.
Music Sales Corporation
257 Park Avenue South, New York, NY10010, USA.
Music Sales Pty Limited
120 Rothschild Avenue, Rosebery, NSW 2018, Australia.

Order No. AM958485
ISBN 0-7119-8005-5
This book © Copyright 2000 Wise Publications

Written by Joe Bennett.
Edited by Sorcha Armstrong.
Music processed by Digital Music Art.
Additional research by Jill Warren.
Thanks to Paul Morris and Basira Ward.

Book design by Phil Gambrill.
Cover design by Michael Bell Design.
Illustrations by Andy Hammond.

Picture Research by Nikki Lloyd.
All text photographs courtesy of
London Features International, except:
Bach (p4 & 24), Minstrels (p8), Lute Player (p9),
Vivaldi (p10), Handel (p10), Mozart (p25) &
Triangle Player (p35) - Mary Evans Picture Library;
Hank Williams (p19), Andrew Davis (p22), The Cardigans (p36),
Yehudi Menuhin (p52), Bob Dylan (p68) &
Django Reinhardt (p83) - Redferns;
Harpsichord (p11), BBC Symphony Orchestra (pp32-33),
Violin (p34) & Roland Keyboard (p38) - Performing Arts Library;
Martin guitar (p15), Fender Stratocaster guitar (p37) - Balafon Books;
The Beatles (p29) - Rex Features.
Additional photographs by George Taylor.

Printed in the United Kingdom by
Printwise (Haverhill) Limited, Haverhill, Suffolk.

Your Guarantee of Quality:
As publishers, we strive to produce
every book to the highest commercial standards.
The music has been freshly engraved and the book has
been carefully designed to minimise awkward page turns
and to make playing from it a real pleasure.
Particular care has been given to specifying acid-free,
neutral-sized paper made from pulps which have not
been elemental chlorine bleached.
This pulp is from farmed sustainable forests and
was produced with special regard for the environment.
Throughout, the printing and binding have been
planned to ensure a sturdy, attractive publication
which should give years of enjoyment.
If your copy fails to meet our high standards, please
inform us and we will gladly replace it.

Music Sales' complete catalogue describes thousands
of titles and is available in full colour sections by subject,
direct from Music Sales Limited.
Please state your areas of interest and send
a cheque/postal order for £1.50 for postage to: Music Sales Limited,
Newmarket Road, Bury St. Edmunds, Suffolk IP33 3YB.

www.musicsales.com

# Introduction 5
# The History of Music 6

# The Composers...

# Musical Instruments 32

# The Music...

# Outro 92

Johann Sebastian Bach (1685-1750), the father of modern music, the...

# Music Theory - What's The Point?
## or "Can't I just sit down and play?"

One of the most common things you'll hear musicians say is "I can play all right, but my theory's no good". Some players even seem to take a pride in their lack of knowledge, saying they "do it by feel" and that their music comes "straight from the heart".

This doesn't happen in any other profession. You'd be alarmed if you hired a plumber who said "I've got plenty of tools, but I really hate water", or if you got on an aeroplane and the pilot announced "I think I can probably get us there, but I don't understand all these dials in front of me".

Music theory isn't anything magical or frightening – it's simply a set of rules and symbols that help us to understand more about the music we hear. In this book you'll find everything you need to get by in music theory, including a crash course in music notation, a rough guide to the instruments, profiles of the major figures in music history, plus essential facts about the most important styles.

*It's Easy To Bluff... Music Theory* gives you an unfair advantage over other musicians. It's an immoral, cheating, deceitful, unethical and deceptive way of improving your knowledge. But it will put you one step ahead of the next bluffer in the gig queue...

# The Five Uses of Theory

**READING MUSIC:** Some musicians spend hours trying to learn pieces all the way through. If you can read music, you've got a constant reminder of how the piece goes sitting right in front of you.

**WRITING MUSIC DOWN:** Why waste time showing people how to play your stuff when you can just hand them a piece of paper? If you write your music down, you only have to do it once.

**COMPOSING MUSIC:** If you know about stuff like chord construction, melodic phrasing, arpeggio usage and polyrhythms, you'll have an idea how the music is going to sound *before* you play it, thus saving time for the all-important creative stuff.

**IMPROVISING MUSIC:** Improvising is just composing on the spur of the moment. If you can hear whether a chord's major or minor, or identify the intervals in a bass part, you'll find it easier to come up with ideas at speed.

**HEARING MUSIC:** It amazing how differently you listen to music when you've got some theory behind you. In short, you understand what you're hearing.

# Classical Music – What you need to know

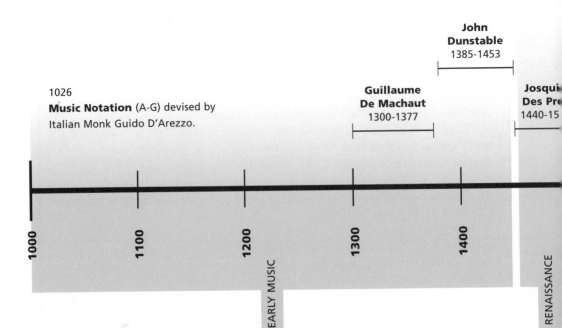

**Before we start here, let's get one thing straight – only plebs use the term 'classical' to describe classical music. Oops.**

Anyway, the reason for this is that 'Classical' music (capital 'C') means the specific period between 1750 and 1820, the time of Mozart and Haydn. So we've got a problem straight away – what do you call music played by orchestras with violins and stuff? 'Orchestral' isn't always accurate, if we're just talking about a string quartet or solo piano, 'Serious' music implies it's somehow better than Pop, Rock or Jazz, 'Traditional' means you get it confused with folk...

No-one's found a good term for it yet, so for the rest of this book, I'm going to use the term 'classical' – just watch for the capital 'C', OK?

On the following pages you'll see a brief description of each musical era, with the essential bluffer's facts about each – when was it, who were the important people, what happened, and what the music sounded like. I've also included a 'knowledgeable fact' about each period so you can *really* impress those in the know...

John
**Dunstable**
1385-1453

1026
**Music Notation** (A-G) devised by
Italian Monk Guido D'Arezzo.

**Guillaume De Machaut**
1300-1377

Josqui
**Des Pre**
1440-15

1000    1100    1200    1300    1400

EARLY MUSIC                          RENAISSANCE

# Timeline – 1000 years in two pages

Below the line you'll see the main musical
eras that you'll hear people talk about.
Above are the major composers
from that time.

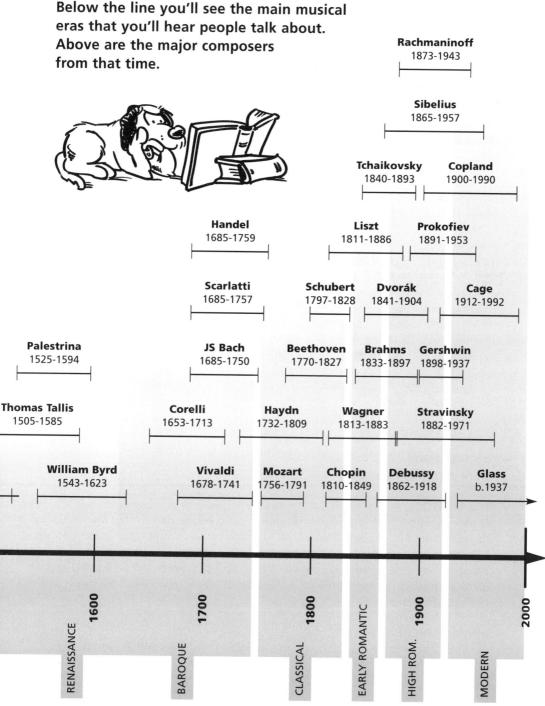

**Rachmaninoff**
1873-1943

**Sibelius**
1865-1957

**Tchaikovsky**
1840-1893

**Copland**
1900-1990

**Handel**
1685-1759

**Liszt**
1811-1886

**Prokofiev**
1891-1953

**Scarlatti**
1685-1757

**Schubert**
1797-1828

**Dvořák**
1841-1904

**Cage**
1912-1992

**Palestrina**
1525-1594

**JS Bach**
1685-1750

**Beethoven**
1770-1827

**Brahms**
1833-1897

**Gershwin**
1898-1937

**Thomas Tallis**
1505-1585

**Corelli**
1653-1713

**Haydn**
1732-1809

**Wagner**
1813-1883

**Stravinsky**
1882-1971

**William Byrd**
1543-1623

**Vivaldi**
1678-1741

**Mozart**
1756-1791

**Chopin**
1810-1849

**Debussy**
1862-1918

**Glass**
b.1937

1600
1700
1800
1900
2000

RENAISSANCE
BAROQUE
CLASSICAL
EARLY ROMANTIC
HIGH ROM.
MODERN

# Early Music

**WHEN:**
1000-1450

**DEVELOPMENTS:**
**Guido d'Arezzo** invented the system of calling the notes by letter names A-G.
Parallel harmony was used (almost always parallel 5ths and octaves). Start of
**polyphony** (literally meaning 'many sounds') – i.e. several vocal or instrumental
lines playing together, creating harmony. Treble clef in use from about 1200.

**WHO TO NAME-DROP:**
**Guido d'Arezzo**, **Léonin** (earliest polyphonic composer), **Pérotin** (his successor),
**Moniot d'Arras** (songwriting monk) and **Guillaume de Machaut** (advanced
medieval polyphonist).

'The Beverley Minstrels' with flute, lute, violin and other wind players (artist unknown)

**INSTRUMENTS:**
Voice, lute, zither, tambor, organ, crumhorn, serpent.

**THE MUSIC:**
Monks chanting with lots of natural church echo (Gregorian chant). Monks doing
the same thing in parallel 5ths. Very long, slow vowels with simple organ backing.
Folk material used simple major and minor scales. Each piece of music stayed in
the same key. The **motet** was popular from the 13th century (it's a vocal-based
piece in which different words are sung with different rhythms at the same time
to create polyphony).

**KNOWLEDGEABLE FACT:**
For most of the Early music era, people stuck to harmonies which used octaves,
4ths, and 5ths. No 'black' notes were used. Which is why, today, we call the interval
between C and G a 'fifth' even though there are 7 semitones in it.

# Renaissance

**WHEN:**
1450-1600

**DEVELOPMENTS:**
Because the plague had just been in town, people paid the church to dedicate religious **Masses** to them, ensuring God's protection. It also kept a good number of composers in work. Polyphony really started to get going, and lots of musical 'rules' on harmony and melody were written down and studied. The **madrigal** (non-religious song in multiple vocal parts) and the **chanson** (voices with one or more instruments) appeared.

**WHO TO NAME-DROP:**
**Guillaume Dufay, Josquin Des Pres** (Flemish polyphonic composers), **Palestrina** (Italian mass composer) **Byrd** and **Tallis** (English madrigals).

**INSTRUMENTS:**
Different lutes, lyres (harp-like hand-held instrument), viols (similar to the violin family, but fretted, and tuned in 4ths), citterns. Crumhorns and other wind instruments which would eventually become flutes, piccolos, bassoons and oboes continued to develop. The harpsichord and organ were the only keyboard instruments.

**THE MUSIC:**
Songs/madrigals were more likely to be in English, or sometimes Italian. Complex harmonies were created by interweaving vocal lines (this is called **counterpoint**). The religious **Mass** was still going strong.

**KNOWLEDGEABLE FACT:**
The first opera, *La Dafne* by **Jacopo Peri**, was performed right at the end of the Renaissance era, in 1597.

'Masked Lute Player' (artist unknown)

# Baroque

**WHEN:**
1600-1750

Antonio Vivaldi

**DEVELOPMENTS:**
This is when the music theory we use now really started to take form. **JS Bach** started writing in **equal temperament** (see opposite page). Polyphonic harmony could now change key at speed. Masques and dance music became popular. The **minuet** was the hip dance everyone was doing. Also, despite the fact that many of the great composers (**Bach, Vivaldi** and **Handel**) did a great deal of work for the church, non-religious music started to thrive, notably the **opera**.

**WHO TO NAME-DROP:**
**JS Bach** is the main one, but **Monteverdi, Vivaldi, Handel, Scarlatti,** and **Purcell** are all big Baroque names. **Pub quiz trivia: Bach, Scarlatti** and **Handel** were all born in the same year, 1685.

**MUSIC TO MENTION:**
Greatest hits of the era include: **Handel's** *Messiah* (which was an **oratorio** – a religious opera without staging); **JS Bach's** *Well-Tempered Clavier* and *Brandenburg Concertos*; **Vivaldi's** *Four Seasons*.

**INSTRUMENTS:**
The Baroque era brought in **concerto grosso** –a small bunch of soloists of equal importance, with an orchestral 'backing band' featuring a **continuo** (bass and harpsichord - pictured opposite - effectively improvising from a chord sheet). Listen out for violins and cellos, trumpets (without valves at this stage), recorder, oboe and bassoon. The church organ and choir were still around, of course, but compositions were more complex, so virtuoso players became more common. The piano and kettledrum/timpani first appeared around this time. Any music you hear with a 'strings section' (violins, viola, cello and bass) is likely to be Baroque or later.

George Frideric Handel

**THE MUSIC:**
More chord changes (by the end of the era, unlimited key changes), and incredibly complex polyphony. Two-part compositions without chord 'backing' were common – the interweaving lines would suggest chord changes. Orchestras started to get bigger. **Operas** started to become popular. If you hear people talk about chorales/chorale preludes, cantatas, fugues, and minuets, that'll be Baroque.

**KNOWLEDGEABLE FACT:**
**Bach** famously walked 250 miles in ten days to see the virtuoso organist **Buxtehude** play. Now *that's* dedication...

**Equal temperament** means the ability for an instrument to sound equally in tune whatever key it plays in. Although we take it for granted now, composers before the Baroque era could only write music that stayed very close to a few musical keys, due to the way the harpsichord and other instruments were tuned.

# Classical

**WHEN:**
1750-1820

**DEVELOPMENTS:**
Polyphonic music was starting to get a bit much for some people, with all those tortuous interlocking melodic lines. People wanted *tunes*. So along came the **solo concerto** (solo instrument with the whole orchestra as backing band). This was also the first time that the **symphony** made its appearance – music for large orchestra without any specific soloist.

The posh and wealthy started hiring composers or players to make music in their homes, which led to **chamber music** (pieces for small groups, e.g. string quartet, piano quintet).

**Opera** really started to make its mark in the Classical era because the orchestras were larger and, most importantly, music became important to a *lot more people*.

**WHO TO NAME-DROP:**
**Mozart** (see page 25), **Haydn**, **JC** and **CPE Bach** (sons of the late **JS**), plus **Schubert** and **Beethoven** (you can bluff a lot with old Franz and Ludwig because they had a foot in both Classical and Romantic eras).

**MUSIC TO MENTION:**
Any of **Mozart's** greatest hits, including **operas** *The Marriage of Figaro*, *The Magic Flute*, *Don Giovanni*; **symphonies** (*Prague no. 38, G minor no. 40*); and any **concerto** (pick your instrument – he wrote solo concertos for piano, violin, flute, clarinet, horn, the lot).

Other top tracks of the time include works by **Schubert** – *Trout* Quintet, *Death And The Maiden* symphony; over 600 **Lieder** (songs), and **Haydn** – mainly known for symphonies (104 of them!).

**INSTRUMENTS:**
The piano was in regular use by all – its ability to play chords, melody and polyphony combined with dynamics was a revelation. **Clarinet** and **trombone** appeared on the scene. Orchestra was standardised into four sections – strings, brass, woodwind and percussion.

**Franz Joseph Haydn**

To this day, clarinet players are sometimes treated as 'upstarts' by some die-hard traditionalists (well, their instrument is only 250 years old…)

**THE MUSIC:**
Melody was a big deal to the Classicists. They generally kept it simple (often 4-bar chunks), and arranged so it was well out in front, which is why lots of the 'classical' tunes most of us know are from this period. The underlying chords were often simple, sometimes as basic as I and V (see page 78).

The dynamics of music changed too – **crescendo** (getting louder) and **decrescendo** (getting softer) were regularly used for full orchestra. So if you hear a piece with constantly changing loud and soft bits, but a great tune, it's probably Classical.

**KNOWLEDGEABLE FACT:**
According to musical folklore, **Mozart**'s mum used to get him out of bed in the morning by playing only the first seven notes of the major scale on the harpsichord. He would get so frustrated with the unresolved 'melody' that he had to get out of bed and play the final note…

**Franz Schubert**

The Clarinet - *only* 250 years old…

# Romantic

**WHEN:**
1820-1910

**DEVELOPMENTS:**
As most of the instruments were hardly different from the Classical period, the major changes were musical. Music became more expressive and expansive, with greater variation in harmony, texture, dynamics and tempo. Middle-class people were becoming more regular concert-goers, meaning music-making wasn't just for the aristocracy.

Piotr Ilyich Tchaikovsky

Composers started to write **Programme Music** – music that would be used to tell stories, with instruments representing characters, or just music that was supposed to be *about* something (the night, the sea, love etc).

And **opera** went bonkers. Stage sets got bigger, works became longer, louder and more dramatic, opera houses were built to seat hundreds, and performers generally waved their arms about more.

Generally, there was a feeling of 'anything goes' – composers started looking backwards as well as forwards by incorporating folk music of their own and other countries, as well as older musical styles such as the polyphony of the **Renaissance**.

**WHO TO NAME-DROP:**
**Beethoven** (later stuff only, please!); **Liszt, Berlioz, Brahms, Puccini, Verdi, Wagner, Mahler, Tchaikovsky, Rimsky-Korsakov, Elgar, Dvořák, Vaughan Williams.**

**MUSIC TO MENTION:**
Lots of Romantic tunes have found their way into our lives – **Johann Strauss**' *The Blue Danube Waltz*, **Verdi**'s *Aida*, **Wagner**'s *Ring Cycle* 'musical drama' (he wouldn't use the 'O' word).

## INSTRUMENTS:

As before, really, but with some refinements. The valve trumpet made the brass section capable of a lot more detail and accuracy, and the tuba gave deeper, fatter sounds to its low end. The saxophone was invented (but took a long time before it was accepted properly into the orchestra). The steel strung guitar arrived in the USA around 1850 but no-one in the orchestra noticed (they still haven't, by the way).

## THE MUSIC:

Bigger, longer and UNCUT! If you wanted the entire last section of your symphony to feature two huge chords getting louder and louder (**Beethoven**) you could. If you felt that two hours for an opera was *just too short* (**Wagner**) then you could add a few. A few days, that is. If you just *knew* your piece needed 30 violins all playing the same melody (**Vaughan Williams**) then no-one was going to stop you.

Johannes Brahms

The melodies were still noticeable and memorable, but more complex, with less reliance on simple background chords. The orchestra still used dynamics, but the range was even greater. Towards the end of the era, composers such as **Wagner** and **Liszt** were starting to question whether you had to use regular chords and tunes anyway...

c.1850 Martin 'Stauffer' with curly headstock and abalone inlay

## KNOWLEDGEABLE FACT:

Scores from the period often avoided simple tempo markings like *andante* (walking pace) and *largo* (slow), opting instead for more emotional suggestions like *dolente* (weeping) and *appassionato* (passionately). Romantic by name...

**Gustav Mahler**

# Modern Age a.k.a. 20th Century

**WHEN:**
1910-current

**DEVELOPMENTS:**
Music of the Modern Age (it was called 20th Century until very recently!) is the most difficult to categorise, because musical change has happened so much faster in the last 100 years. For a start, recordings could be made, so not all music needed a score.

In some cases, composers tried to get away from melody and harmony altogether (**atonalism**). World and Folk music, used to a great extent by the Romantics, was used as a basis for composition by **Stravinsky** and **Bartók**. And Europe was no longer necessarily the home of all creativity. Americans such as **George Gershwin**, **Aaron Copland** and **Charles Ives** started to incorporate jazz into popular compositions.

And then there were the really mad ones. **John Cage** composed for wind-up gramophones, pianos with bits of screws and nails stuck into them, and his famous *4'33"* which consisted of a silent piano. **Harry Partch** divided the octave into 43 microtones and built instruments that could play the scale he'd invented. Composers tried anything and everything to get away from the music of the past.

Since the 1950s, we've had electronic music. Whereas the rock and pop industry has generally used music technology to create fairly ear-friendly sounds (so it sells!), the classical world has often used it to challenge traditional musical ideas. Music for microphone inside pig's intestine is not unheard of.

**WHO TO NAME-DROP:**
Tricky, this, because you need to make sure you don't say them all in the same breath. In rough groups of style, try dropping in **Bartók, Sibelius, Vaughan Williams** (nationalists); **Schöenberg, Webern, Stockhausen** (atonalists), **Aaron Copland, George Gershwin, Samuel Barber** (er, Americans), **Terry Riley, Steve Reich, Philip Glass** (minimalists). Other significant figures include **Stravinsky, Boulez, Messiaen** and **Satie**.

**Igor Stravinsky**

**MUSIC TO MENTION:**
**Stravinsky's** *Rite of Spring*, **Schöenberg's** *Five Pieces For Orchestra*; **Copland's** *Fanfare For The Common Man*; **Satie's** *Gymnopedie*; **Cage's** *4'33"*; **Terry Riley's** *In C*.

**INSTRUMENTS:**
Apart from the ridiculous-looking sousaphone, there weren't any changes made to the instruments of the Romantic orchestra. The gramophone was used in compositions (and later the tape machine, CD and DAT, all of which have been used in performances). The Theremin was invented in Russia (it's an electronic instrument which is played by moving your arms around without touching it). And of course, the synthesiser, MIDI sequencer, and multi-track studio have radically changed the way music is composed.

**THE MUSIC:**
**Atonal** music sounds like it isn't in a key and doesn't have a 'tune' or 'chords' as **diatonic** music does (the idea is that your ear's not being 'told' how to feel by major and minor chords etc).
**Avant-garde** or **Experimental** music can sound like anything, but commonly doesn't use regular instruments or even musical notes. **Minimalism** is actually quite listenable to the average person, as it frequently consists of mesmerising loops which change very gradually.

Jean Sibelius

**New Romanticism**
leans to the music of the 19th century, with its swooping arrangements and emotional content.

**KNOWLEDGEABLE FACT:**
Because **atonal** music doesn't give us anything to 'latch on to' as listeners, its effect can be quite frightening. For this reason, it was used by horror film soundtrack composers of the 1960s to create tension – just watch any old Hammer **Dracula** movie to hear atonal music in action.

Béla Bartók

# Popular Music - The Bare Facts

Pop Music started in 1955. Sure, before that we had best-selling Jazz records. In the 1920s there were blues, ragtime and country singers who were selling thousands of records. If you want to get really picky, you could argue that there were sheet music song sales in the 1800s. And the English folk song's been around for centuries...

Still, 1955 was when Billboard magazine started to publish their Top 100 singles chart. It was also the year that **Bill Haley**'s 'Rock Around The Clock' hit number 1. A year later, **Elvis Presley** appeared on the scene.  So that's when it started. Awright?!

## Theoretical pop

And since that time, it's had almost no effect whatsoever on music theory. Notation still follows the same conventions it did 300 years ago (all right, so bands use chord charts, but so did JS Bach). Chord structures rarely get beyond four or five chords, and hardly ever feature key changes. And everything's in 4/4 time.

So why is popular music so important? The simple reason is that it allows people who don't know anything about theory to write and record music. Basic chords and single-key melodies form the backdrop for more important things like production, vocal style and lyrics.

The good news, from a bluffer's point of view, is that you don't need as much music theory to get by in the pop world as you do in the classical one. A good understanding of chord construction, time signatures and keys is really all you need to become a great popular musician (along with talent, of course!).

On these pages, I've listed some of the important styles in popular music's history, with notes on what each one sounds like, famous names and classic tracks.

**Elvis Presley**

# Jazz

**Louis Armstrong**

**GOLDEN YEARS:** 1920-1955

**SOUND:** Improvised music, usually in small groups, where players 'take a solo' over given chord changes (later, larger bands created the 'Big Band Sound' of the 1930s). Typical instruments – voice, clarinet, saxophone, trumpet, guitar, piano, upright bass, drums.

**THEORY:** Chords are always more advanced than in most other pop music (jazz uses 7ths, 9ths, 13ths and loads of **altered** chords). Jazz frequently features cover versions – these are known as 'standards'.

**FAMOUS NAMES:** Louis Armstrong, Benny Goodman, Charlie Parker, Miles Davis, John Coltrane, Ornette Coleman, Herbie Hancock

**CLASSIC TRACKS:** What's important is not so much the song but the *version*. So it's **Django Reinhardt**'s version of 'Ain't Misbehavin'', **Louis Armstrong**'s version of 'Summertime', etc.

# Country

**GOLDEN YEARS:** 1940s+

**SOUND:** Small bands of guitar/s, bass, drums, often with piano, pedal steel guitar and big harmony vocals. Sometimes violin. Regular verse/chorus structure.

**THEORY:** *Very* basic chords – sometimes just I, IV and V (see page 80). Usually 4/4 time. Solo 'emotional' vocal with big harmonies in places.

**FAMOUS NAMES:** Jimmie Rodgers, Hank Williams, Johnny Cash, Willie Nelson, Tammy Wynette. More recently Garth Brooks and Shania Twain.

**Hank Williams**

**CLASSIC TRACKS: Tammy**'s 'D.I.V.O.R.C.E', **Patsy Cline**'s 'Crazy', **Kenny Rogers**' 'Lucille', **Dolly Parton**'s 'I Will Always Love You'.

# Rock 'n' Roll

**Chuck Berry**

**GOLDEN YEARS:** 1955-65

**SOUND:** Guitar, bass and drums, sometimes with piano. Snare on beats 2 and 4 of the bar. Hi-hat plays 8 to the bar. Sometimes with a swing beat, sometimes straight (see page 49). Aggressive style and fast tempo. Evolved from Rhythm & Blues.

**THEORY:** Use the I, IV and V of blues chord sequences and speed them up. Keep the chords sparse and the bass pumping those 8s. Guitar solos frequently use 'double-stops' (i.e. two notes at a time).

**FAMOUS NAMES:** Elvis Presley, Chuck Berry, Bill Haley

**CLASSIC TRACKS: Bill Haley**'s 'Rock Around The Clock', **Elvis Presley**'s 'Heartbreak Hotel', **Chuck Berry**'s 'Johnny B. Goode'.

**TRAINSPOTTER'S CORNER:** Rock 'n' roll drummers often came from swing and jazz backgrounds. On some of the early stuff you can hear the entire band rocking away in straight 8s, while the drummer completely ignores their groove and puts a jazz 'swing' into the kit part. Get hip, daddi-o.

# Soul

**James Brown**

**GOLDEN YEARS:** 1965-1975

**SOUND:** Basically, chart-friendly pop music for black America. Sweet, emotional vocals with multiple backing harmonies. Guitar, bass and drums rhythm section often included Hammond organ, electric piano, sax and brass section.

**FAMOUS NAMES:** Ray Charles, Sam Cooke, Aretha Franklin, James Brown

**CLASSIC TRACKS: Smokey Robinson**'s 'Tears of a Clown', **Marvin Gaye**'s 'What's Going On', **James Brown**'s 'Get On Up (I Feel Like Being A Sex Machine)'.

# Rock

**GOLDEN YEARS:** 1965-1980 (but still going strong)

**SOUND:** Fuzzed-up guitars, and usually slightly slower tempos than its predecessor, Rock 'n' Roll. Male vocals are usually very high (middle C and above). Deep, solid bass parts.

**THEORY:** Rock brought us the 'power chord' – a two-part chord using only the root and 5th of the scale – it misses out the major or minor 3rd. The guitars frequently play these on the lower strings.

**FAMOUS NAMES:** Jimi Hendrix, Cream, The Who, Van Halen, Nirvana, Oasis

Jimi Hendrix

**CLASSIC TRACKS: Jimi Hendrix**'s 'Hey Joe', **Led Zeppelin**'s 'Stairway To Heaven', **Nirvana**'s 'Smells Like Teen Spirit'. But there are thousands of others...

# Dance/Rap

**GOLDEN YEARS:** 1987-2000 (but started back in 1979)

**SOUND:** Musicians playing machine-like grooves, or machines playing musician-like grooves. Less emphasis on the 2&4 back beat of Rock. Focus on the beat/groove rather than traditional lyrics, tunes and chords. Frequent use of samples of other musicians or of spoken word.

**THEORY:** Everything in 4/4 time, but usually based on a 16-to-the-bar groove rather than the straight 8s of Rock or the swinging feel of Jazz. Recent styles (Drum & Bass, Jungle) have pushed tempos beyond even Rock 'n' Roll – 180BPM and higher.

**FAMOUS NAMES:** Grandmaster Flash, Run-DMC, Public Enemy, The Beastie Boys, The Prodigy, Fatboy Slim

**CLASSIC TRACKS: Grandmaster Flash & Melle Mel**'s 'The Message', **Public Enemy**'s 'Don't Believe The Hype', **Fatboy Slim**'s 'Praise You'.

**Run-DMC**

**Andrew Davis conducting The Last Night Of The Proms.** You have the conductor, the instruments and the players – all you need now is a piece to play

# The Composers

## Bite-size biogs

In this section you'll find an instant guide to five of the most influential and prolific composers and musicians in history. These are the ones you absolutely must know something about in order to converse with history buffs.

For each composer, I've included some basic **biographical information**, notes on **style and era**, and (more importantly) what their **contribution** was to the history of music. These are the important things to know if you are to convince people that you know what you're talking about.

If you're actually asked to prove that you've heard the composer's work, you'd be stuck without the quick and easy **'finest hour'** reference. This is an essential song or piece for you to mention (but not necessarily the best-known - it can sometimes pay dividends to bluff your way by showing you listen to the obscure stuff).

You should have no trouble getting recordings of these, and it's essential to have actually *listened* to something by each of these composers.

Finally, it's always useful to have a few oven-ready opinions up your sleeve. In each biography, I've included an 'instant opinion' (usually ambiguous enough to cover all situations) and an 'acceptable criticism'. If you're cool enough to criticise one of the greats, you can consider yourself to be a 'black-belt' bluffer.

# Johann Sebastian Bach

**DATES:** 1685-1750

**WHO?** Seminal German composer of the Baroque era

**BACKGROUND INFO:** First important gig was as church organist and chamber musician to the **Duke of Weimar** (bluff tip – "The Weimar period" – pronounce it with a V or you'll show yourself up). Failed to get the promotion he wanted, so took a job with the **Prince of Anhalt-Cöthen** ("The Cöthen period" – are you getting it now?) where he wrote his famous *Brandenburg Concertos*. After five years he became a cantor (director of music) for **St Thomas's Church** in Leipzig (you guessed it – "The Leipzig years"). Spent the last 27 years of his life there and wrote most of his large-scale works.

**CONTRIBUTION:** Apart from writing better polyphonic music than anyone else around at the time, he also started writing for the 'equal tempered' keyboard (see page 11). Large-scale choral works and incredibly complex multi-part fugues in later years cemented his reputation as the most important composer of the Baroque era, and one of the most influential musicians who ever lived.

**FINEST HOUR:** The *Brandenburg Concertos* are very listenable and are still played regularly on film and TV today. The *Well-Tempered Clavier* is his most influential because of its use of equal temperament. The *Mass In B Minor* is a huge classic in every sense of the word 'huge'.

**INSTANT OPINION:** "The most significant musician who ever lived."

**ACCEPTABLE CRITICISM:** Some people find his music so technically perfect that they say it lacks emotion. Warning – make sure you've heard a *lot* of Bach before you try this viewpoint in a bluffing situation.

# Wolfgang Amadeus Mozart

**DATES:** 1756-1791

**WHO?** Austrian composer of the Classical era

**BACKGROUND INFO:** Began as a child prodigy – started composing before the age of five, and was a touring virtuoso by the time he was six (it's just as well he started early because he died aged 35). By the time he was 13 he'd written concertos, symphonies and several operas. He described his music as existing in his head – for Mozart, composing was simply a process of committing the ideas to paper. In the 1770s he worked for the **Archbishop of Salzburg**, but after a disagreement, quit and went freelance in Vienna, taking commissions wherever he could find them. Worked extensively for **Emperor Joseph II** but was given lowly tasks such as composing dances for the court. Spent the last ten years of his life fighting his financial problems, but still managed to create his best work during this period.

**CONTRIBUTION:** Wrote some of the greatest tunes in the classical (and Classical!) world. His final six symphonies are the most significant examples of the form up to that point. Most famous for this operas – he wrote in, and improved on, the three operatic forms of the time – **Opera Buffa** (Italian comic opera); **Opera Seria** (Italian 'serious' opera); and **Singspiel** (German light opera).

**FINEST HOUR:** *Eine Kleine Nachtmusic* is an excellent (and famous) example of his chamber music. Famous operas include *The Marriage of Figaro*, *Don Giovanni* and *The Magic Flute*. His *Piano Sonata in C minor* is still popular with pianists.

**INSTANT OPINION:** "The most perfect melodic composer in musical history."

**ACCEPTABLE CRITICISM:** Died before he could achieve his full potential. That's really the only criticism you'll get away with when it comes to Mozart.

# Richard Wagner

**DATES:** 1813-1883

**WHO?** German operatic composer of the Romantic era

**BACKGROUND INFO:** Apart from a few months of music theory lessons, he was entirely self-taught. Quit Leipzig University in 1833 and took on various jobs in musical theatre. Lived in Paris briefly, where he completed his first two grand operas, *Rienzi* and *The Flying Dutchman*. Started to compose what he called 'Music Drama'. Moved to Zurich in 1849 after becoming involved with revolutionaries in Dresden. For four years, he stopped composing and wrote books instead, including his famous *Opera and Drama* in which he documented his theories about theatre composition. Some of his works were so large-scale that there was nowhere that they could be performed. His epic *Ring of the Nibelung* (four operas in one) was first performed in 1876, after a theatre was specially built for him by **King Ludwig II**.

**CONTRIBUTION:** Opera singers in pointy Viking hats, warbling and shouting a lot – you've got Richard to thank for all that stuff. But apart from the staging (and some very dodgy opinions on German supremacy) he's still responsible for some major changes in music. His music features **leitmotifs** (short, recurring phrases which symbolise a person, character, object or idea). He also, incidentally, pushed chromatic harmony and complex chords about as far as anyone had up until then.

**FINEST HOUR:** The *Ring* cycle (four operas in one) is his biggest, but *Tristan and Isolde* and *The Flying Dutchman* are equally famous. And shorter.

**INSTANT OPINION:** "The single most important figure in the development of opera."

**ACCEPTABLE CRITICISM:** After his death, Wagner's music was appropriated by the Nazis as a symbol of all that was great about Germany. But that wasn't *his* fault.

# Louis Armstrong

**DATES:** 1900-1971

**WHO?** American Jazz composer and performer

**BACKGROUND INFO:** Everywhere that early jazz innovation happened, Louis Armstrong was there; New Orleans at the start of the 20th century; Chicago in the early '20s, New York City in the late '20s. Distinctive vocal style and larger-than-life appearance led to the affectionate nicknames "Pops", "Dippermouth" and "Satchmo" (a shortening of "Satchel-mouth"!). During the '20s he played in some of the most influential bands of the era, including **The King Oliver Creole Jazz Band** and his own **Hot Five**. Continued to have success throughout his life, although his later material as a vocalist leans more towards popular entertainment than groundbreaking improvised jazz. Made over 50 films, and was still having top ten hits in the mid-'60s.

**CONTRIBUTION:** As a cornet and trumpet player, he was among the first to play the 'stop chorus', where the band plays one beat and then leaves a gap for the soloist to fill with improvisation. He was an early exponent of 'scat' (improvising a vocal melody using nonsense syllables). And, of course, he was one of the earliest players to 'solo over changes'.

**FINEST HOUR:** Any Hot Five or Hot Seven recording – check out his solos on 'Potato Head Blues' or 'West End Blues' in particular.

**INSTANT OPINION:** "The Godfather of Jazz."

**ACCEPTABLE CRITICISM:** His music became less interesting the more successful he got – 1960s singles (*Wonderful World*, *Hello Dolly*) were great vocal performances, but lacked the excitement of his 1920s work.

# The Beatles

**WHO? John Lennon** (1940-80), **Paul McCartney** (b.1942), **George Harrison** (b.1943) and **Ringo Starr** (b.1940)

**BACKGROUND INFO:** Formed in 1959 out of John Lennon's earlier group, **The Quarrymen**. Original line-up of John, Paul, George and drummer **Pete Best** changed when Ringo Starr was found to be a better drummer. Learned their trade in the nightclubs of Hamburg, but also toured the UK extensively, and got their first record deal in 1962. Early albums were typical of (if substantially better than) 'Beat' music at the time, but Lennon & McCartney soon found their feet as composers, and by their middle period (*Rubber Soul* and *Revolver* albums) were starting to experiment with different song forms and instruments. Their landmark 1967 album *Sgt. Pepper's Lonely Hearts Club Band* is still one of the most important in the history of popular music.

Towards the end of the '60s, band arguments were getting more and more extreme, and this was made worse by the financial problems of the band's own Apple label. They split in 1970, and their final album *Let It Be* was released afterwards. The band had recorded 186 songs during its career, which included 13 full-length original albums. Any hopes of a reunion were dashed when John Lennon was shot in New York in 1980. The remaining three did get back together briefly in the 1990s to record additional parts onto an old Lennon song, *Free As A Bird*.

**CONTRIBUTION:** Until the Beatles, most singers were not singer-songwriters. Their first album was 50% cover versions, but as time went on they added more of their own material until by 1966 every song on every Beatles record was self-composed. But they also made musical changes that are now considered normal practice in pop music. The way many vocal harmonies are arranged owes a lot to The Beatles; recording techniques such as vocal automatic double-tracking were pioneered by them; they even used early Moog synthesisers.

**FINEST HOUR:** Although you'll hear many people praise *Sgt. Pepper's*, it's also worth getting the equally interesting *Revolver* and *Abbey Road*.

**INSTANT OPINION:** "The most important band in popular music history."

**ACCEPTABLE CRITICISM:** They recorded some dross – 1963's 'Hold Me Tight'; 1968's 'Don't Pass Me By'; and 1970's 'For You Blue' are lazy and fairly unmemorable. And they let Yoko sing.

**The Beatles** did more than sell millions of records – they also wrote a lot of the rules that popular music theory still uses today.

# Emergency backup bluffs

Here are the basics on four other influential figures and groups in music theory history. I've included The Atonalists and The DJs because they're great for starting arguments – always a good way of raising your bluffer's profile.

## 1. Ludwig Van Beethoven (1770-1827)

German composer – straddled the Romantic and Classical eras. Hot-housed by his alcoholic father, he became a senior court orchestra member by the time he was thirteen. He was spotted by **Haydn** and moved to Vienna where he composed private commissions for various wealthy patrons. Beethoven is probably best known to other bluffers for being deaf, but he was miserable too. He famously argued with **Haydn**, **Mozart** and several of his patrons. Greatest hits include opera *Fidelio* and several symphonies – the *Fifth* and *Ninth* being the most famous.

## 2. The Atonalists (1920s-50s)

In 1921 **Arnold Schöenberg** (pictured) developed the 12-tone, or serial composing system, as a guaranteed way of making music that deliberately avoided any key centre (**atonal**). Other names to drop include **Webern, Berg, Stockhausen** and **Boulez.** The 12-tone system involves using every semitone of the octave, always played in order without repeating any notes. Do this on several instruments at different speeds, and play some of the bits backwards, and you get the 'scary' music which has since been used in various horror movie soundtracks. It's easy to criticise but lots of the works are very well put together – check out **Schöenberg**'s *Pierrot Lunaire* and *Five Pieces for Orchestra*.

# 3. Jimi Hendrix (1942-1970)

If the guitar is the most important instrument in pop music history, this man is its most important player. Pioneered various guitar techniques including controlled feedback, whammy-bar techniques, fuzz and other special effects, as well as various flamboyant stage antics including setting his guitar alight and playing it behind his head. In true rock style, Hendrix trod the usual path of poor business deals, artistic differences and drug abuse. Classic hits include *Hey Joe*, *Purple Haze* and *All Along the Watchtower*. Died, aged 27, choking on his own vomit as a result of drink and drugs complications.

# 4. The DJs (1985-current)

The term originally meant 'Disc Jockey' – i.e. people who played records. During the late 1980s musicians began to use sections of pre-existing vinyl recordings as part of a band mix – the person who kept the records in time with the band and created 'scratching' effects became known as the DJ. Since then, the term has come to mean anyone who is involved with either playing records, mixing records live to create a 'seamless' sound – usually in nightclubs – or re-mixing records in a studio to create new recordings. Many of the Dance CDs sold now will feature the DJ's name in the song title, to distinguish between different versions of the same song. Names to drop include **The Chemical Brothers, Carl Cox, Paul Oakenfold** and **Fatboy Slim** (both pictured).

# Musical Instruments

**If you're ever going to write music for other instruments, or even if you just want to jam with other players, you need to know a bit about their instruments. In this section, you'll find a brief fact file on every commonly-used classical and rock instrument, together with information on how it's used.**

If you're bluffing your way through with one of these players, it can earn you instant cred if you mention, in passing, something specific to their instrument. If you were talking to a guitarist you might casually say "good job you've got a cutaway, otherwise you wouldn't make the high note in that solo". Or you might tell a drummer "I just love those flams you're playing in the middle 8". And if you can write out a melody in the correct key for an alto saxophone player, you can expect *at least* one free drink during the interval...

Harps

Clarinets
(and Bass Clarinets)

Timpani

Percussion

First Violins

French Horns

# The Orchestra

The picture below shows the placement of all
the instruments within a typical modern orchestra.

**Flutes**
(and Piccolo)

**Bassoons**
(and Double Bassoon)

**Trombones**

**Trumpets**

**English Horn**
(Cor Anglais)

**Tuba**

**Oboes**

**Double Basses**

**Second Violins**

**Cellos**

**Conductor**

**Violas**

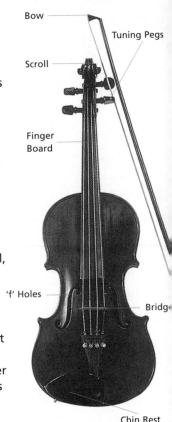

Bow

Tuning Pegs

Scroll

Finger Board

'f' Holes

Bridge

Chin Rest

# Strings

A 'String section' consists of violins (pictured), violas, cellos and double basses. The violins divide into 'firsts' and 'seconds' – the instruments are the same but the first violins generally play higher pitches, with the seconds playing harmony parts. The Strings are tuned, bass to treble, in 5ths (the violin is GDAE, the viola CGDA and the 'cello CGDA an octave lower). The exception is the double bass, which is usually tuned in 4ths i.e. EADG (the same as the bass guitar). Strings can be played with the bow (**arco**) or plucked with the fingers (**pizzicato**).

**PLAYER-WATCH:** String players are generally very genteel, unassuming types. They will normally be polite to you as long as you speak to them in a nice accent. **First violinists** can often get carried away with their own egos (what with being referred to as the 'leader of the orchestra'). **Double bass** players frequently do moonlight shifts at the local jazz club round the corner from the concert hall. For orchestral gigs, they always stick together – that way they can nudge each other if one of them falls asleep during the slow bits.

# Brass

Bell

Valves

Mouthpiece

The 'Brass section' features trumpet, French horn (pictured), trombone and tuba, though other instruments (e.g. Cornets, bass trombones) are added for some pieces. Brass instruments are usually **transposing** instruments, meaning that the notes they read and play are different from the ones we hear (so if a trumpeter plays a C, it actually comes out as a B♭). Confusing? Yes, I know. The reasons are tied up in the history of the instrument and the different ranges that have developed. All these brass instruments except the trombone use valves to get some of the notes – the pushing of the valves changes the length of brass tubing that the air passes through, altering the pitch. In addition, the player uses lip pressure to get higher notes.

**PLAYER-WATCH: Trumpeters** are the lead guitarists of the brass world. They're so convinced of their own importance that they frequently don't even bother to tune up (they think that during the solo sections the audience will assume that *everyone else* is playing flat). **Trombone** players are more like scruffy trumpeters – they generally eat more pies and can usually be caught with a pint of Real Ale next to their music stand (musical fact – you can't hear a belch when it goes down the tubing of a brass instrument while you're playing).

# Woodwind

Reed & Mouthpiece

In an orchestra you'll generally get flute, oboe, clarinet (pictured) and bassoon. Sometimes extra instruments such as piccolo, bass flute, bass clarinet and saxophone are added – generally played by the same people 'doubling' instruments. The clarinet and saxophone are, like the brass, **transposing** instruments, so when they play their 'C', what we hear is a B♭ or E♭. There are three types of woodwind – *non-reed* (recorder, flute, piccolo); *single-reed* (clarinet, saxophone) and *double-reed* (bassoon, oboe).

Science bit – most people think that the sound comes out of the end of a woodwind instrument. Inexperienced sound engineers take note – it comes out *everywhere*, yes, even out of the holes in the side.

Keys

**PLAYER-WATCH:** The woodwind section are notoriously old-fashioned. The **bassoon**, **flute** and **oboe** players know that their instruments go back to medieval times, so they're pretty well in there with the traditionalists. The **clarinet** has been around since the late 17th century, so they just about get away with it in the eyes of the others (though some bassoonists still treat them like young whippersnappers). The **saxophone player** (whose instrument was invented over 150 years ago, remember) is still viewed by the rest of them as an outrageous drug-taking drop-out who's at risk of turning a beautiful *ppp* woodwind passage into a big-band jazz solo extravaganza at any moment.

# Percussion

Bell

There are two types of percussion – *tuned* and *non-tuned*. *Tuned* percussion (e.g. piano, timpani, xylophone, glockenspiel) can produce actual musical notes that we hear as a pitch. *Non-tuned* percussion is generally used for rhythmic ideas or special effects only (e.g. bass drum, snare drum, cymbals, triangle, wind chimes). The xylophone and glockenspiel can actually carry a tune, and their layout is identical to a keyboard, with sharps/flats and naturals as on a piano – you just hit them with beaters rather than pressing a key. There are two kinds of **timpani** (aka **kettledrum**) – those of fixed pitch (which will be tuned to a certain pitch before a concert) and those with pedals, where the player can change the tuning with a foot pedal.

**PLAYER-WATCH:** Let's forget all the drummer jokes for now. If we accept that the hardest part of reading music is the *rhythms* (see page 53), the percussion player has got a pretty tough job. However, bear in mind that one of the most important criteria for a percussionist is being able to count bars of rests accurately. These people can sit for hours simply staring at a line of black rectangles on a score, waiting for the moment when they go 'ting'. With this in mind, never get caught in solo conversation with a percussionist.

Triangle Player

# The Rock Band

There are four, arguably six instruments here, each usually played by a single person (rock musicians don't hang around in groups the same way orchestral players do – if they want more sound they simply turn up the amp).

To begin with, guitar, bass, drums and piano was the standard rock 'n' roll band. Later, the organ and electric piano came along, followed by the synthesiser, which could produce so many sounds that we now just use the catch-all term keyboard player. More recently we've seen the DJ and programmer involved in live performance.

Shown on this page is a typical rock band setup. Generally the vocalist is at the front in the middle, the guitarists and bass players stand to one side, the keyboard player, programmer and DJ go further back near the backline (amplifiers), and the drummer sits at the back. Old joke – how can you tell if the drum stool is level? The drummer drools out of both sides of his mouth at once.

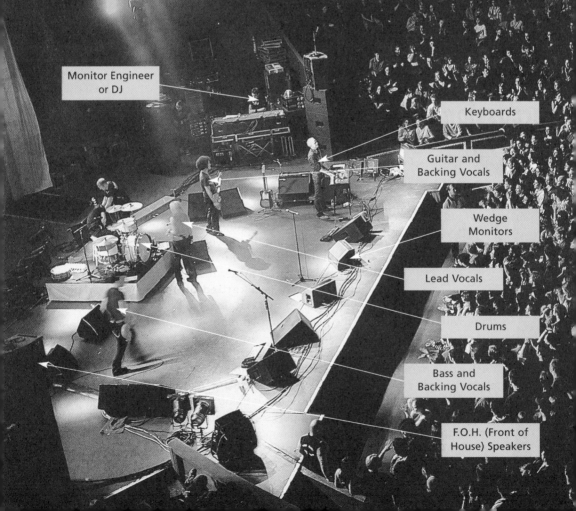

Monitor Engineer or DJ

Keyboards

Guitar and Backing Vocals

Wedge Monitors

Lead Vocals

Drums

Bass and Backing Vocals

F.O.H. (Front of House) Speakers

# Vocalist

Although in the classical world vocalists are formally arranged into pitch-related groups such as soprano, alto, tenor and bass, in pop and rock music the band works around the most comfortable range for the vocalist they've got. So if the singer finds a piece too high or low to cope with, the band will **transpose** the key of the song to fit. Because on-stage volume levels are so high (due in part to the acoustic volume of the drum kit) the singer commonly has some form of monitoring so they can hear themselves. This is usually a speaker facing towards them, or sometimes an in-ear headphone-type device. If you hear a rock singer who's out of tune, or time, when they're singing live, it's usually because of bad monitoring.

Liam Gallagher

**Bluffer's tip** - if you can sing naturally, lead vocalist is the easiest job in rock. You don't have any gear to carry, you don't have any difficult instrumental parts to learn, you get to be the centre of attention, and you receive (at least) as much money as any of the players.

# Electric Guitar

Like its classical cousin, the electric guitar has six strings and is tuned EADGBE. It has between 19 and 24 frets, and tuning pegs to alter the string tension. And there the similarity ends. The electric and acoustic guitar are as different in their own way as, say, the clarinet and saxophone. You could argue that the electric guitar is the more versatile too. The fact that the instrument is amplified means it has an unlimited dynamic range; the options for using effects to alter the sound of the instrument are endless; and the solid construction and steel strings mean that each note sustains for longer than any hollow-bodied instrument.

Getting started as a guitar player is easy – players can learn simple 'box-shapes' on the fingerboard to create credible improvisations with very little experience. Sorry, guitarists, but it's time to own up to all those other players – *you don't know the names of the notes you're playing*. Other instrumentalists never can get their heads around this – but they're just jealous because they picked a difficult instrument in the first place...

Headstock

Tuning Pegs

Nut

Fretboard

Pickups

1956 Fender Stratocaster with 'Sunburst' finish

Tremolo Bar

Pick up Selector

Headstock

Tuning Pegs

Nut

Neck

Scratchplate

Bridge

# Electric Bass

The bass as we know it today was invented by Leo
Fender in 1951. It plays an octave lower than the deepest-
sounding strings of the electric guitar (i.e. EADG) and has a
longer neck due to the increased string tension. Unlike the
upright double bass it uses frets, so the bassist can hit the notes
with perfect accuracy (this is why the first production model
was called the Fender Precision). It's played using three main
techniques – **fingerstyle** involves the player resting their
thumb on the body and plucking the strings with two fingers;
**picked** uses a plectrum; and **slap bass** uses the bone of the
thumb's top joint hitting the strings onto the fingerboard, while
the fingers pull the upper strings away from the fingerboard
and let them snap back.

Sometimes the instrument's range is extended – the 5-string
bass is tuned BEADG, or occasionally EADGC – but for most
rock and pop recordings, the 4-string's 3-octave range is usually
enough. The proper name for the instrument is the 'horizontal
electric fretted bass' because, in terms of tuning and range,
it's just a double bass on its side. But hey, if it looks like
a guitar, feels like a guitar and there's a guitarist playing it,
it's probably because the band can't find a proper bass player.

# Keyboard

Thanks to advances in sampling and synthesis
technology, the keyboard as we know it today
can make any sound imaginable, including every other instrument
in the band. But in rock and pop it commonly plays one of four or
five roles. The **pad** is a soft, warm sound which is used to 'pad out'
the arrangement with gentle chord backing. **Mono lead lines**
emulate the monophonic synthesisers of the 1960s and 70s (used
for high melodies or basslines). Keyboard instruments that can be
recreated include the **Hammond Organ**, **Electric Piano** and
**Clavinet**. Instrument simulation (where the player is used to fill
the role of acoustic instruments like **violins** or a **brass** section) is
generally done for reasons of convenience or finance. And it's
particularly good for special effects – the keyboard is still the
easiest instrument to use for triggering samplers and synthesisers.

Keyboard players are frequently the most musically-educated in
the band. They're also the most technically-minded. Many of them,
however, spend so much time convincing themselves that their
sample library sounds 'just like a real orchestra' that they start
to believe that keyboards really can replace other instruments.
This condition is referred to as Self-Delusional Acoustic Aural
Awareness Disorder (i.e. SAAAD).

# Drums

There are five basic elements to a drum kit – bass drum, snare drum, tom-toms, hi-hat (two cymbals pushed together) and cymbals. Tom-toms (in rock-speak just 'toms') come in various different sizes which can be either *mounted* (usually on the bass drum) or *floor* (with their own legs). There are two types of cymbals – *ride* cymbals are used for rhythms, typically played 4 or 8 to the bar, and *crash* cymbals are used for the noisy bit. Drums are played with *sticks*, *brushes* or occasionally *rods* (lots of thin sticks strapped together which feel like normal sticks but aren't so loud).

A good kit player is several percussionists in one – it's not the hitting of the drums that's difficult, it's co-ordinating them all at the same time. Drummers are usually responsible for the count-in of a track, and (unless machines are being used) they keep the tempo consistent throughout, playing the role of conductor, metronome, rhythm arranger and five percussionists all at the same time. So next time you make a drummer joke, remember that they can probably change ten light bulbs at once...

Ride Cymbal

Crash Cymbal

Hi-Hat Cymbals

Mounted Tom

Floor Tom

Snare Drum

Bass Drum

# Music Notation

**If you want to remember something, you write it down. In the same way, if you want to remember the notes in a piece of music, you write them down. And if you want to play someone else's music accurately, you read it from notation.**

We commonly notate music in one of three ways – **chord chart**, **full notation** or **graphic score**. Graphic score is a way of notating music using pictures, lines and shapes, generally used for experimental compositions. It doesn't tell you what notes to play or when to play them. Or anything about keys, chords, scales, sharps and flats. If you're the kind of bluffer who can read a graphic score accurately you're probably also the kind of bluffer who can describe a glass of wine as "cheeky, with a hint of pensive vulgarity". This book does not deal with graphic scores.

# Chord chart

Shown here are some of the common symbols you'll see in chord charts and what they mean. For more on what the chord names mean, see page 69...

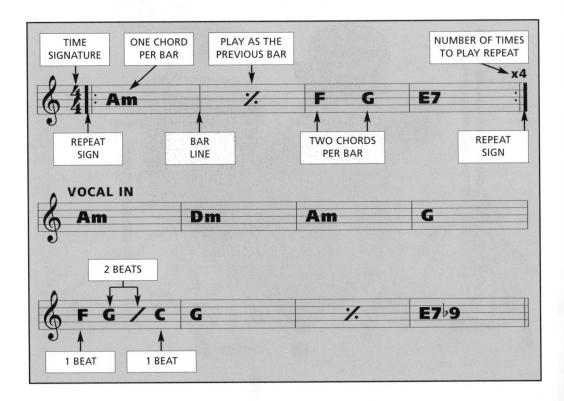

# Full notation

...and here are the names of the elements of full notation. Don't worry if some of the terms are new – they're fully explained later on in the book.

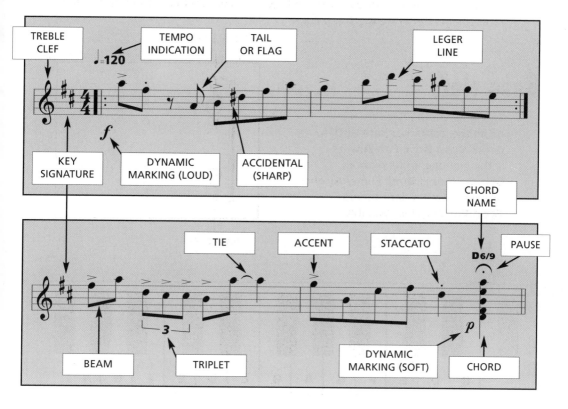

# The stave – remembering the pitches

We write music on a **stave** (also called a **staff**). It's exactly like a graph, in this case showing only **pitch** (vertical) and **time** (horizontal, going left to right as with the written word). Because different instruments have different ranges (see page 32), we use **clefs** to show roughly which range we're working in. There are four of these, but in almost every piece of music you see, you'll only ever need to work with two – treble and bass. **The notes of the treble and bass clef are shown over the page.**

 # Bluffing Tip

If you can remember the names of the notes on the lines, you don't need to know the notes in the spaces, as it's just going to be the adjacent note above or below, thus saving you half of the memory work.

# Treble clef

Music teachers have for years been saying **E**very **G**ood **B**oy **D**eserves **F**avour (or **F**ootball or **F**un or whatever) as a way of remembering the notes on the lines of the treble clef. I've always preferred my versions **E**at **G**reen **B**roccoli (**D**ie **F**ast) or **E**lephants **G**enerate **B**ig **D**eep **F**arts.

# Bass clef

The notes on the lines
(from the bottom up) are GBDFA.
**G**reen **B**uses **D**rive **F**ast **A**lways
is the dull one, or how about
**G**eordie **B**lokes **D**rink **F**unny **A**lcohol,
or back on a flatulent theme
**G**reat **B**ig **D**ogs **F**art **A**udibly.

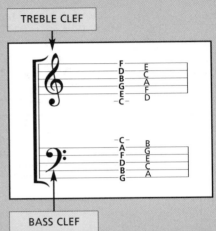

TREBLE CLEF

BASS CLEF

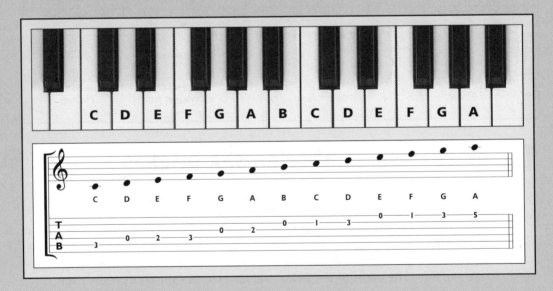

# Leger lines

If a note goes too high or low for the clef, we simply draw in more lines to extend the clef for that note. These are called **leger lines**, and just as with the regular stave lines, notes can be above the line, on the line, or below the line.

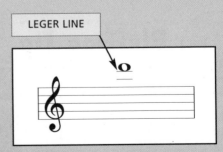

LEGER LINE

# Key Signatures

There are 12 notes or *semitones* in the musical scale, but we usually only play 7 of them in a section of music. To decide exactly *which* ones are right and wrong-sounding, we can avoid trial and error by using a key signature.

## Explanation

The musical scale always has the notes ABCDEFG in it, regardless of what key you're in. It's just that some of the notes need to be sharpened or flattened to keep them 'in key'. The key signature tells us which ones we should change.

### 1. USING SHARPS IN KEYS

Here, we're in the key of G major (which has one sharp – an F#). This means that every time you see a note on the F line (top line) you should actually play F#. So this example is played F# F# E F# C B.

### 2. USING FLATS IN KEYS

In this example, all the Bs (middle line) should be played as flats. So here we'd play F G A B♭ C. This is the key of F major.

### 3. MORE FLATS

In the key of E♭ major, this example would be played A♭ B♭ C. Only the C note would be unchanged, because it's not sharpened or flattened in the key signature.

## Never together

Sharps and flats never occur together in the same key signature. You're always in either a 'sharp' key or a 'flat' key.

# Major Keys

Shown here are all the major keys and which sharps and flats they use.

C major

G major

D major

A major

E major

B major

F# major

C# major

# Bluffing Tip

If you find it difficult to remember the 'sharp' keys, here's a trick.
Look for the sharp on the right, and go one note higher. That's the name of
the key you're in. So if you're in the two-sharps key, look to the sharp on
the right (C#) and go one note higher. You're in D major.

C major

F major

Bb major

Eb major

Ab major

Db major

Gb major

Cb major

# The Wheel of Keys

Most musicians don't actually READ the key signature – they just make a note of how many sharps and flats there are in it, and that tells them the key.

So if the music is in a major key and you see three sharps you're always going to be in A major, for example. Which means you don't need to remember exactly which sharps and flats are in each key, just how many.

This diagram is called the Circle of Fourths and Fifths. Counting clockwise, the notes on it go up in fifths. Counting anti-clockwise, they go up in fourths. Yawn. BUT, if you start at the key of C (no sharps or flats) and go clockwise one step, you get to G, which has *one* sharp. Go another step and you get to D, which has *two* sharps, and so on. Do the same thing anti-clockwise and you get the 'flat' keys of F, B♭, E♭ etc.

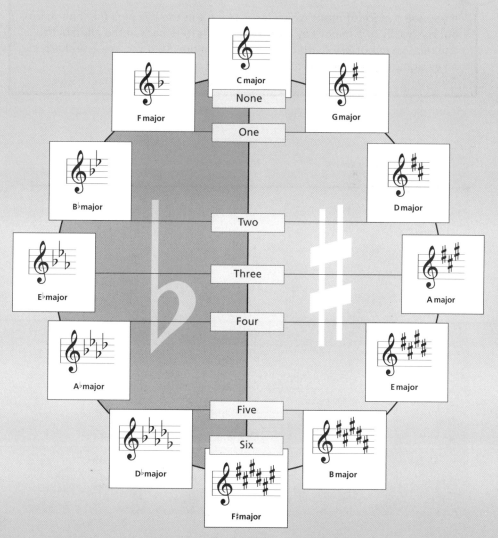

# Minor Keys

Every major key has a relative minor which has the same key signature – i.e. it uses the same notes.

If you know that the music is in a minor key (if there are chord names written, the first one will usually be minor) simply count two letters backward in the alphabet from the major key signature.

# For Example

If you see a piece of music which looks like it's in the key of G (i.e. one sharp), but is actually in a minor key, just count two letters back in the alphabet to E. The relative minor key (with one sharp) is E minor. So if you see one sharp in a key signature, you're in either G major or E minor.

| Number of ♯s or ♭s | Major key | Minor key |
|---|---|---|
| No sharps or flats | C major | A minor |
| ♯ | G major | E minor |
| ♯♯ | D major | B minor |
| ♯♯♯ | A major | F♯ minor |
| ♯♯♯♯ | E major | C♯ minor |
| ♯♯♯♯♯ | B major | G♯ minor |
| ♯♯♯♯♯♯ | F♯ major | D♯ minor |
| ♭♭♭♭♭ | D♭ major | B♭ minor |
| ♭♭♭♭ | A♭ major | F minor |
| ♭♭♭ | E♭ major | C minor |
| ♭♭ | B♭ major | G minor |
| ♭ | F major | D minor |

# Rhythm Notation

**So now that we know what the names of the notes are, we need to know how fast or slow to play each one, and where they fall in relation to each other.**

Rhythm notation uses a combination of **note values** (i.e. how long a note lasts) and **rests** (i.e. the length of the gap between notes) to give us all this information.

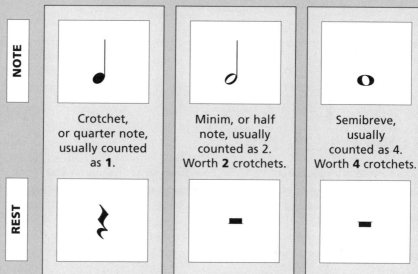

**NOTE**

Crotchet, or quarter note, usually counted as **1**.

Minim, or half note, usually counted as 2. Worth **2** crotchets.

Semibreve, usually counted as 4. Worth **4** crotchets.

**REST**

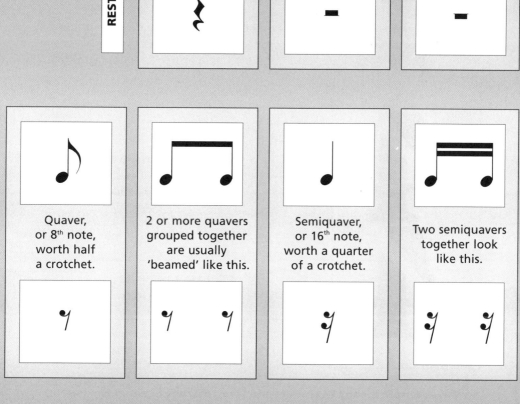

Quaver, or 8th note, worth half a crotchet.

2 or more quavers grouped together are usually 'beamed' like this.

Semiquaver, or 16th note, worth a quarter of a crotchet.

Two semiquavers together look like this.

# Tied and dotted notes

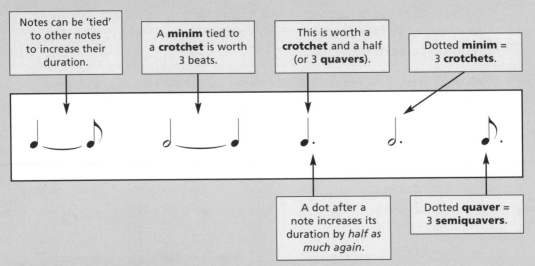

Notes can be 'tied' to other notes to increase their duration.

A **minim** tied to a **crotchet** is worth 3 beats.

This is worth a **crotchet** and a half (or 3 **quavers**).

Dotted **minim** = 3 **crotchets**.

A dot after a note increases its duration by *half as much again*.

Dotted **quaver** = 3 **semiquavers**.

# Time signatures

Some music teachers try to explain time signatures by saying "look it's really easy – just think of fractions in maths". Aaaaaargh! Forget the maths, let's talk about *music*. We need to know *how many* beats in a bar, and *what kind* of beats they are.

That's all a time signature is. It tells you how many beats, and whether they are slow, medium or fast note values.

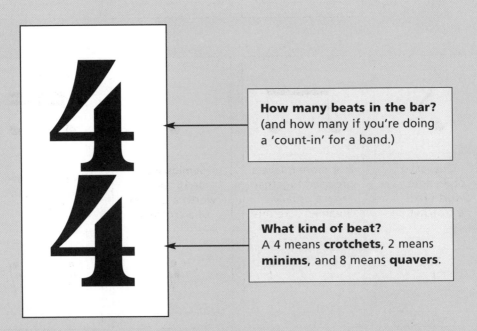

**How many beats in the bar?** (and how many if you're doing a 'count-in' for a band.)

**What kind of beat?** A 4 means **crotchets**, 2 means **minims**, and 8 means **quavers**.

**So this example means that there are four crotchet beats in the bar.**

# Simple and compound time

If you were 'counting-in' a rock band, you'd most likely go "1, 2, 3, 4" because most rock music is in 4/4 time. 4/4 time is an example of a **simple** time signature, not because it's easier than the others, but because every count is a whole beat.

In **compound** time, we divide each beat up into sub-beats, so some beats feel stronger than others. So for a song in 6/8 (six beats, and each of them a quaver) we'd actually count the band in "**1** *and a* **2** *and a*". There are six syllables in your count-in (one for each quaver), but the stronger beats are the **1** and **2**. Examples of songs in compound time include the '60s classic 'Unchained Melody', the nursery rhyme 'Humpty Dumpty' or the **Manic Street Preachers'** song 'Design For Life'.

 # Rule of Thumb

If the bottom number in the time signature (i.e. the kind of beat we're using) is a **2** or a **4** (i.e. a minim or a crotchet) then we're in simple time. If it's an **8** or a **16**, we're in compound time.

# Swing grooves and straight time

If you speed up 12/8 time ("1 *and a* 2 *and a* 3 *and a* 4 *and a*"), then one of the quavers (the "and" beat) becomes unnoticeable.

Try saying the 12/8 count to yourself (go on, no-one's looking!) and gradually accelerate until you can't say the 'and' fast enough. Drop it out but keep the same rhythm. You've created what's called a 'swing', or 'shuffle' feel. Examples of shuffle grooves include most blues and trad jazz, the nursery rhyme *Pop Goes The Weasel*, and the **Elvis Presley** hit *Hound Dog*.

 # Bluff-speak

When you hear a musician talk about 'swung 8s' they mean eighth notes (i.e. quavers) played with a swing (i.e. every first quaver is slightly longer than every other one). This is also technically known as a 'broken triplet'. The opposite of 'swung 8s' is 'straight 8s' (i.e. every note is played exactly evenly).

# Guitar Notation

The guitar is the world's most popular instrument. But formal notation doesn't give all the information guitarists need (e.g. fret positions, fingerings for chords, string bends and so on). And besides, most guitar players really hate to read music.

So over the last 100 years or so, special forms of notation have been developed to make things easier for players. Here are a few of the most common.

## Tablature

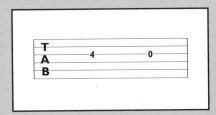

**Tablature** is like the guitar turned on its side – the lines represent the strings (the headstock of the guitar is on the left, meaning the bottom line is the bass E string). The numbers show you which fret to press (a zero means play the open string without fretting the note). Normally, you see tab with treble clef written above it.

| Advantages | Disadvantages |
|---|---|
| Shows fret positions. Easier to learn than regular notation. Works equally well for chords or solo lines. | Doesn't tell you the note names. Doesn't show rhythmic values. Doesn't help you to understand the instrument. |

## Fretbox

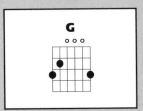

A **fretbox** is the guitar upright – the headstock is at the top and the vertical lines represent the strings. Circles show you where to put your fingers, and above any strings which aren't fretted you'll see an O (meaning play the open string) or an X (meaning don't play that string at all). Fretboxes are usually used to show chords, though sometimes can be adapted to notate scale shapes too.

| Advantages | Disadvantages |
|---|---|
| Shows fret positions. Easier to learn than regular notation. Shows the chord as a shape, which is how the player thinks of it. | Doesn't tell you the note names. Doesn't show rhythmic values. Can only be used for chords or scales. |

# Chord charts

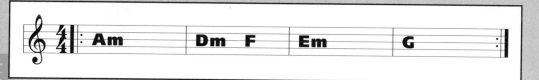

A **chart** is simply a list of chords with barlines in it (see page 40). Despite the relative lack of information it is the most popular way for writing music down in rock and pop. Charts can be as simple as two or three chords scribbled on the back of an envelope, or they can be complete notation with barlines, Coda markings and repeats, missing only the treble or bass clef element.

| Advantages | Disadvantages |
| --- | --- |
| Easier to learn than regular notation. Quick to write out and understand. Gives lots of freedom for players to improvise. | Usually, not very detailed. Doesn't show rhythmic values. Can only be used for chords. |

# Classical notation

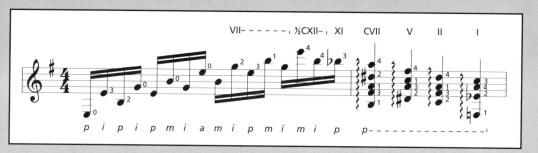

Basically treble clef with knobs on. Rather than try to reinvent the wheel, classical guitar players decided to stick with normal notation and write in the extra bits. So the Roman numerals refer to the fingerboard position, the small numbers next to the notes show the fingering, and the letters **p, i, m** and **a** show which fingers to pick with (i and m stand for index and middle finger, and p and a stand for, er, thumb and… the ring finger).

| Advantages | Disadvantages |
| --- | --- |
| The only system that gives all the information. Covers chords, melody and rhythms. Complex parts can be written out in full. | Difficult to learn. Even more difficult to sight-read. Not as useful in rock & pop guitar parts. |

**Yehudi Menuhin** - If only he'd had a copy of this book, he wouldn't

# How To Read Music

Music reading is an acquired skill, just like playing your instrument. And in that same way it can take years of practice before you're really good at it.

However, you'll progress a lot faster when you're learning if you remember three things.

- **The more music you read, the better your reading gets**
- **Reading music is more about reading rhythms than pitches**
- **You can read anything if the tempo is slow enough**

There will never be a magical day when your reading suddenly 'happens'. You'll just get gradually better at it until one day you'll look at notation just like you look at this book – you understand what's there without thinking about it.

# Sight-singing

If you possibly can, sing in a choir. Doesn't matter whether it's hymns, gospel or opera. This is a fantastic quick way to improve your music reading, because it reminds you that when the notes go **up**, the music goes **up** in pitch. Although that seems obvious, you're not teaching yourself; you're teaching your subconscious brain. The rhythms of the piece will come to you easily (a lot of the time you're singing the same rhythm as someone else in the choir anyway). And, of course, if you get lost, you can always mime for a few bars until you pick it up again. Only try this in a really BIG choir.

# Singing tips

- **Stand next to someone who's better at sight-singing than you are – you'll be surprised how quickly you improve.**
- Follow the direction of the notes up and down.
- **Guess the right note if you're not sure. Even if you're wrong, your subconscious brain will force your voice to sing a musically related note. This really works if you show enough confidence.**
- Go for it! If your singing is weedy and apologetic, it will come out flat. And that's when everyone else *really* starts to notice.
- **Don't worry too much about reading the rhythms. With choral material, a lot of the time you're singing the same rhythm as everyone else anyway.**

# Reading Rhythms

To read rhythms you need to start by thinking of them really slowly. You should always have a mental metronome running in your head, reminding you where the pulse is, and where the off-beats (i.e. the beats between the pulses) are.

On this page I've supplied some examples of single-bar rhythms to help you to develop a sense of pulse. Each example gets gradually more difficult as more off-beats and rests are used. Try clapping or tapping these rhythms as you count.

Right, so that's a **minim** (worth 2 beats) and two **crotchets** (worth 1 beat each). Simply count "1 2 3 4" under them to give you the pulse. Obviously, if the first note lasts for two beats, the other two will be on beats three and four. Easy!

Here, the first note is only one beat long, but there's a rest on the second beat. Keep counting through the rest, but just don't play anything. Not too tough...

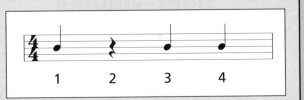

Now we've introduced **quavers**, or eighth notes. But don't panic – all it means is that there are two notes played for every one you count. To fill the gaps in the pulse, let's say "and" between the counts. Doesn't hurt yet?

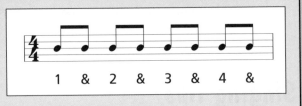

Now, on one of the downbeats (in this case, the count of "3") there's a **quaver** rest. Start this one very slowly. Your counting should stay even, even though your playing misses out a note. When you have learned the phrase, play it at speed and it will sound completely natural – not like reading music at all.

# Repeats

Most music features repetition of some sort. Repeat symbols (shown as ||: and :|| )
are handy because they save the composer notating things twice.

From the player's point of view, when you see a repeat the music reading part
of your brain can relax slightly – you're playing something you've done before.
On this page there are two examples of common repeats. In each case it's shown
as a chord chart because it's easier to see which bars are being repeated, but all
of the theory applies to any kind of notation. The top example shows what you'd
see in the notation; the bottom example shows what you'd actually play.

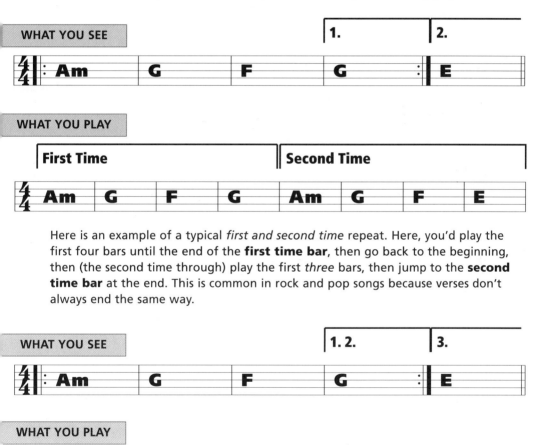

Here is an example of a typical *first and second time* repeat. Here, you'd play the
first four bars until the end of the **first time bar**, then go back to the beginning,
then (the second time through) play the first *three* bars, then jump to the **second
time bar** at the end. This is common in rock and pop songs because verses don't
always end the same way.

And if you can have first and second time, why not third and beyond? This is a great
example of how repeats can make things easier - just look at how complicated the
full version looks!

# Form Notation

Sometimes we want to do more than just repeat – maybe we want to jump
to another place in the music, or go back to the beginning, or jump to a coda
(ending section or outro). For this we use form (i.e. structure) notation.

# Typical DS Al Coda

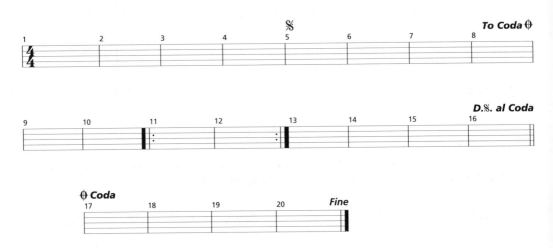

This is an example of form notation in action. Rather than put
actual music in there, I've numbered each bar to make it easier to
understand which bars we're talking about. Follow the example
through as you read the text, counting bar by bar, and it should
become clear how these 'jumping' instructions actually work.

Start from the beginning of the piece and play through bars 1-8 inclusive,
making a mental note of where the ℅ is and where the instruction **To Coda** appears
(but don't do anything about them at this stage. Carry on through bars 9 and 10.
Play bars 11 and 12, then play bars 11 and 12 *again* (this is just a regular repeat).
Now play bars 13-16. **D.℅. al Coda** tells you to go back to the ℅ sign, so jump back
to bar 5. Now that you've had your **Al Coda** instruction, you should jump to the
coda section (bars 17-20) when you reach the end of bar 8.

Now you're at the Coda, just play the last four bars and stop where it says *Fine*
(pronounced "Fee-nay").

You'll sometimes see the phrase **DC al Coda**. These are even easier – instead
of jumping back to the ℅ sign, you jump right back to the beginning.

**There are seven score markings you need to learn...**

| Abbreviation | Latin name | What it means |
| --- | --- | --- |
| DC | Da Capo | Go back to the beginning of the whole piece |
| DS | Dal Segno | Go back to the ℅ sign, wherever it is in the piece |
| Al Coda | Al Coda | Go to the Coda (or) get ready to go to the Coda |
| ⊕ | Coda | Used to mark where the Coda is, or where to jump to the Coda |
| ℅ | Segno | Used to mark a particular place you should jump to in the score |
| DC al Coda | Da Capo Al Coda | Go back to the beginning then jump to the coda whe you see the words Al Coda or the ⊕ Coda sign |
| D.℅. al Coda | Dal Segno Al Coda | Go back to the ℅ sign then jump to the coda when you see the words Al Coda or the ⊕ Coda sign |

# Myths about music reading

- **Music reading is the same as sight-reading**
  Lots of people, even pro session players, don't play completely 'cold' from unseen music. Rather, they look at the notation to show them how the piece goes, then 'teach their fingers' how to play it. Then when it comes to performance or recording, they simply use the score to remind them how to play a piece they already know.

- **Music reading takes the 'feel' out of a performance**
  Yes, sometimes, but only if you're not a very good reader. If you read well enough, you won't be concentrating solely on the notation, giving you time to think about the emotional aspects of your performance.

- **Music reading is just for 'classical people'**
  Lots of players (usually rock guitarists) say this, and it's true that rock bands rarely use formal notation. But if everyone in your band reads and you can communicate by jotting ideas down for each other, you'll save loads of rehearsal time. Not to mention the fact that you'll be able to play songs from books that you don't even know.

- **It all goes by too fast – I'll never be able to read at that speed**
  Start slowly and build up speed. I mean REALLY slowly. How about one note every 5 seconds? Stupidly easy, huh? All right, how about one note every second? Bit more difficult? If you gradually do this with every new piece, the speed will come to you eventually.

- **If I learn to read, I won't be able to improvise any more**
  Only non-music readers say this. It's a lame excuse. Think about it – if you learn a new word do you forget all the old ones? Of course not – so why should new musical information stop you remembering what you already know?

# Scales

Oh, you mean warm-up exercises? Those things you have to do for piano exams? Well, if that's all you're using scales for you're missing out bigstyle. In this section, we'll look at how scales are formed, and how we use them in music theory.

# What is a scale?

A scale is a series of (usually 7) notes which follow a certain pattern of **tones** and **semitones**. A scale is defined not so much by the notes in it, but by the spaces (intervals) between each note.

# How to build a major scale

To illustrate, imagine you're playing all the white notes C to C on a piano.

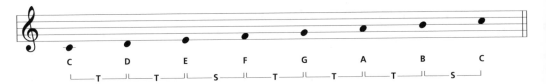

Take a look at the intervals between the notes. Note that the space between C (the **root**) and D (the **major second**) is a **whole tone** (i.e. there's a note in between the two). The space between, say, E and F is just a **semitone** (no black note between the white ones).

This means that although the white notes *appear* to be equally spaced, it's actually an illusion created by the grouping of black and white notes on the keyboard. So when we play all the white notes C to C, the intervals *between* the notes are Tone, Tone, Semitone, Tone, Tone, Tone, Semitone. I've abbreviated this TTSTTTS.

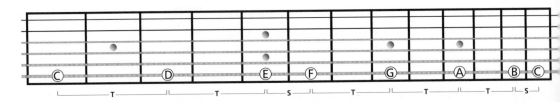

This is actually much easier to see and understand if you try to play a major scale on one string of a guitar. This example starts on a note of C at the 8th fret on the sixth (thickest) string.

# The major scale

Major scales are the most important in Western music because they define the key. If you play music that features only white notes, we'd usually describe this as 'playing in C' i.e. the scale of C major.

The intervals between the notes of the major scale (see previous page) are TTSTTTS. The musical names we give to the notes that occur in the major scale are shown below.

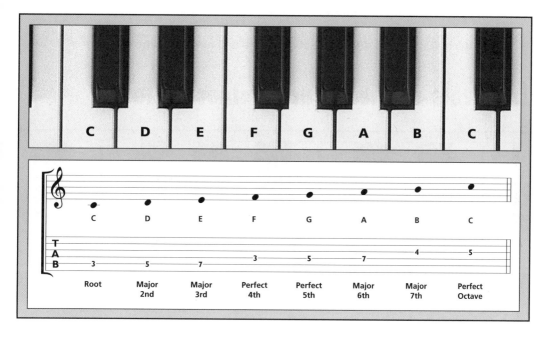

# Intervals of the major scale

All of this major scale theory is the same whichever key you're in. The sharps and flats in other keys only exist in order to keep these major key intervals sounding right in different keys (indeed, that's why we have key signatures). For more on this see page 63.

 # Sound

Major scales generally sound bright, happy and predictable. Try playing a C major scale and inserting any black note – it'll make you cringe!

# The Minor scale

If we *alter* the major scale pattern of tones and semitones we can create a minor scale. In this example, I've dropped the third, sixth and seventh notes by one semitone, creating a pattern of TSTTSTT.

For some of the interval names, the word major is replaced by the word minor – so our scale goes Root, major second, *minor* third, perfect fourth, perfect fifth, *minor* sixth, *minor* seventh, perfect octave. Note how the 'perfect' intervals (the notes of C, F and G in this case) are unaltered regardless of whether we're playing a major or minor scale.

The technical name for the scale shown here is **C natural minor.**

# Intervals of the natural minor scale

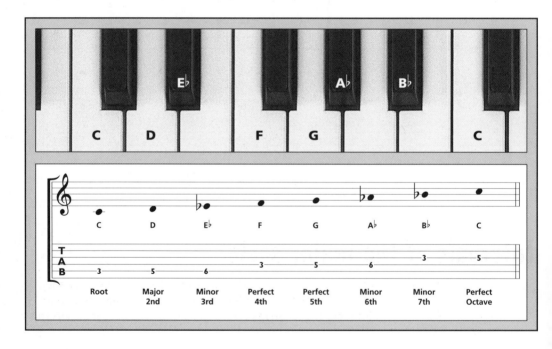

| Root | Major 2nd | Minor 3rd | Perfect 4th | Perfect 5th | Minor 6th | Minor 7th | Perfect Octave |

 # Sound

Minor scales generally sound darker and more intense than major scales. The defining characteristic of a minor scale is its flattened (or 'minor' third note). Listen for the difference between major and minor thirds – they've got a completely different feel.

Dire Straits' **Mark Knopfler** – minor scale man.

# Minor scales in other keys

Here are two more examples of natural minor scales. Note that the A minor example is all white notes, but that all-important interval pattern (TSTTSTT) is intact. When a minor scale uses the same sharps and flats as a certain major scale, this is called a **relative minor**. So the scale of A minor is the relative minor of the scale of C major.

# A natural minor scale

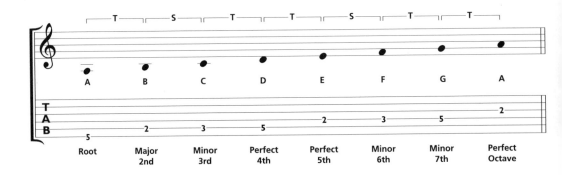

# E natural minor scale

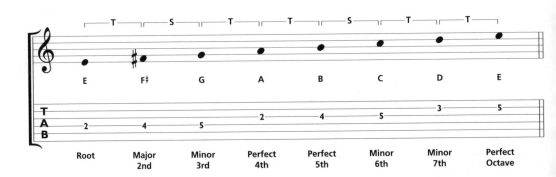

# Scales And Key Signatures

Now that we know how to construct a major scale from its intervals (see page 58) let's relate that to our understanding of key signatures. Everybody knows the sound of the major scale by feel. If you don't believe me, find a keyboard and prove it to yourself.

# Try this

Play all the white notes G to G – sounds kind of wrong, doesn't it? Now try making every 'F' that you play into an F♯ – i.e. raising it one semitone. Now it all sounds OK. Now would it surprise you that the key of G major has one sharp in it? Can you guess which sharp? Course you can.

# Now try a really tough one

Start on a note of E on the keyboard and try to build a major scale by ear. Once you've figured it out so it sounds 'right', take a look at how many sharps you used. If you got four, give yourself a large pat on the back with whichever hand isn't in knots on the keyboard. Now check how many sharps there are in the key of E major (page 45). Congratulations – you've used your natural aural skills to support your music theory.

 # Guitarists' Corner

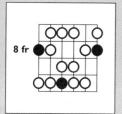

8 fr

Guitarists have it REALLY easy when it comes to key signatures, because you can play any major scale with a single fingerboard shape if you know the names of the notes on the bass E string.

Simply use the two-octave fretbox shape below (shown here starting on a note of C at the 8th fret). Play it in whatever key you need by moving the whole shape up or down the fingerboard so it starts on a different note.

The black circles indicate root notes (i.e. notes of C). If you play the shape accurately, all the sharps and flats of the key will naturally fall under your fingers. Try it!

# Modes

Modes are 7-note scales which each create a different feel, or 'mood'. Some of them sound major and some minor. The reason they're grouped into one category is that they can all be constructed from the major scale.

# What do you mean?

If we play all the white notes C to C, we know that it creates the pattern of tones and semitones we call the major scale, right? But what if we play the white notes D to D? This doesn't create any sort of major scale because the pattern of tones and semitones is different, and we haven't used the key signature to compensate. The pattern of intervals which is created when you use the major scale in this way is a **mode**.

**So all modes use the white notes, right?**
Not necessarily. All music can be **transposed** into any key (and will therefore start to use black notes), and modes are no different. You can play a mode in any musical key as long as you keep its Tone/Semitone pattern intact. Here's an example of how a mode is constructed:

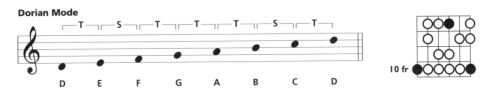

Dorian Mode

Here, I've constructed the **Dorian** mode (the name given to the mode that is created by the white notes D to D). Its formula of intervals works out, as you can see, at TSTTTST. Guitarists, of course, can play this in any key simply by moving the Dorian box shape to any fret.

# All the Modes for guitarists

**Ionian**   **Dorian**   **Phrygian**   **Lydian**   **Mixolydian**   **Aeolian**   **Locrian**

Here are all seven modes shown as moveable box shapes for guitar. No fret position is given, because the black note is the root – i.e. the note name you need to know if you're going to play the modes in every key. Each mode is shown in two octaves, and the root is marked each time it appears.

# All the Modes

Below, on the left, I've shown all the modes in white note keys so you can compare their construction. To get a better idea of how they sound, though, I've also shown them with a root note of C, on the right.

# Pentatonics

**Most scales, as we know, have seven notes. A pentatonic is simply a scale with five notes. We get rid of the ones that are considered to be musically 'less important'. Effectively, we use the best-sounding notes.**

There are two types of pentatonic, major and minor. They're both shown here with a root note of C so you can try them out and hear the difference.

## C major pentatonic

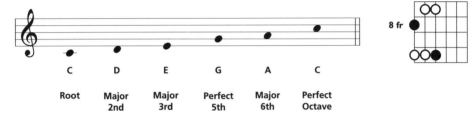

| C | D | E | G | A | C |
|---|---|---|---|---|---|
| Root | Major 2nd | Major 3rd | Perfect 5th | Major 6th | Perfect Octave |

## C minor pentatonic

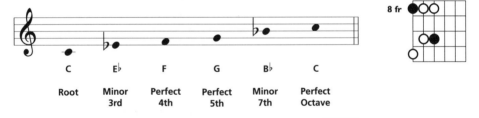

| C | E♭ | F | G | B♭ | C |
|---|---|---|---|---|---|
| Root | Minor 3rd | Perfect 4th | Perfect 5th | Minor 7th | Perfect Octave |

## What's the point?

Pentatonics are great scales because they use the 'best' notes – i.e. the ones that are least likely to sound 'wrong'. That's why musicians use them to improvise solos – most of the time they're unlikely to hit a wrong note. With pentatonic scales, *everything* sounds cool.

## Cosmic Pentatonic

Listen to Jay Kay of **Jamiroquai** singing – every melody he comes up with is almost entirely pentatonic.

# Artificial Scales

Some scales are artificially altered by composers or improvisers for a specific musical purpose. Here's a selection of the most common.

## Melodic minor

This is a bizarre scale, and almost impossible to use in composition or improvising because it uses different notes descending from the notes it uses ascending. It was probably invented by a sadistic piano teacher in the mid-1800s primarily to upset grade 1 piano students. This scale is pure evil and should be avoided at all costs.

## Harmonic minor

This one is a bit more useful because it works well with some types of chord change. Developed around the Baroque era, it's more often used in classical music than in rock and pop. Sometimes sounds vaguely 'Eastern' if you try to improvise with it.

## Whole tone scale

If you play a scale with no semitone intervals in it (i.e. only tones) this is what you get. Primarily used in jazz to improvise over augmented fifth chords.

However many chords you know, sometimes you can say it all with

# Chords

When you play two or more different notes at the same time, you're creating a chord. Chords can be two-note (diads), three-note (triads) or can contain four or more notes (extended). They are usually made up of notes from a scale (see page 79), but for this chapter we're going to look at them in isolation.

## Uses of chords

**AS CHANGES:** If a band is playing around an agreed chord sequence ('playing changes') this is a flexible enough structure to allow for some improvisational freedom within it. This is how jazz bands improvise.

**AS ACCOMPANIMENT:** If you've worked out your sequence to be played as a backing track, chords can be played over and over in rhythm as part of a band mix. This is what rhythm guitarists do when they're strumming.

**MULTIPLE PARTS:** If you've got lots of instruments that can only play one note each (say, a brass band) you can write a different note of the chord for each player. That way, you create harmony as a group, even though you're not using chord-playing instruments (or you could just hire a sampler!)

**CHOIRS AND BACKING VOCALS:** If you apply the 'multiple parts' principle to the human voice, you get a choir. In most unaccompanied choral music there is an identifiable chord structure, even though no single instrument is playing a chord.

**INVISIBLE CHORDS:** If you write your melodies carefully enough, your audience's brain will fill in the backing chords and hear the music as if it has a major or minor feel even if there are no chords present. Listen to any solo version of the hymn *Amazing Grace* or Suzanne Vega's unaccompanied recording of 'Tom's Diner' for further proof.

 ## Chord tips for keyboard players

- Don't always play the chord as root-third-fifth – it gets boring. Try putting the third or the fifth at the bottom of the chord.
- Try arpeggiating the chords – i.e. playing the notes one at a time.
- You don't always need 3-part chords. Sometimes one or two notes is enough, especially if you're in a big band.
- If you're a chord-based piano player, chances are you're in the habit of playing octaves with the left hand. Ask yourself – do I really need both those notes?
- Do you have to use a strings sound on *everything*?

# Major Triads

These are easy to work out if you know your key signatures. If you want to play a chord of D major, simply think about the scale of D and use its root, third and fifth note (technical names – root, major third and perfect fifth).

On this page I've notated six of the most common major chords in **root position** (this means that their root note is played at the bottom of the chord). Compare any sharps or flats used in the chord with the key signature of that name (page 43) and you'll start to get an idea of how chords, keys and scales are all related.

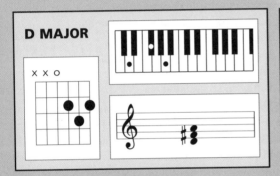

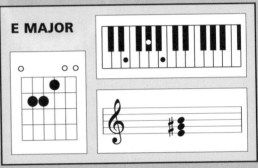

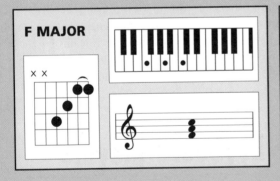

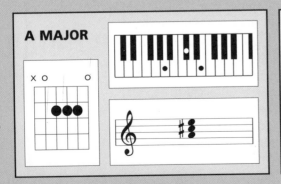

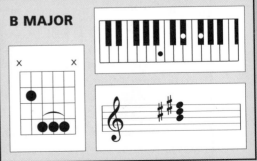

# Minor Triads

On this page, I've shown the minor version of every chord shown opposite.

Note that each chord has been made minor simply by dropping the middle note (i.e. the 'major third') down one semitone. Major third becomes minor third. So major chord becomes minor chord. Obviously!

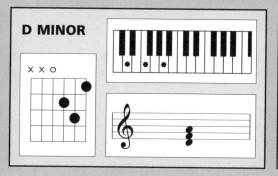

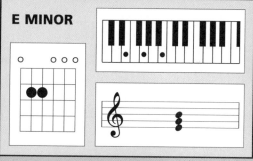

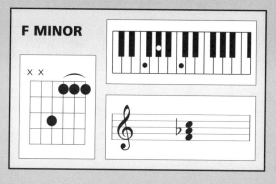

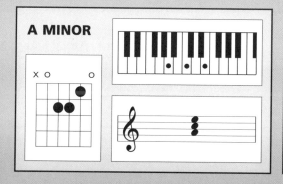

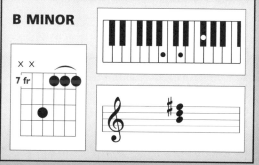

# Seventh Chords

There are four kinds of seventh chords you need to know. Three of them appear all the time in lots of different styles of music. One appears only in **James Bond** films and bad 1980s cop shows.

In each case, you keep the root and fifth of the chord exactly as for a regular major or minor chord, but sometimes flatten the third or seventh to make them minor intervals. All examples are shown here with a root note of C, and I've also shown how they are commonly notated in chord charts.

## Sevenths in a pie!

The diagram shows roughly how common the different types of sevenths are in recorded music, together with some examples of their use.

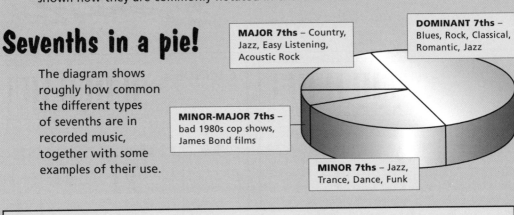

MAJOR 7ths – Country, Jazz, Easy Listening, Acoustic Rock

DOMINANT 7ths – Blues, Rock, Classical, Romantic, Jazz

MINOR-MAJOR 7ths – bad 1980s cop shows, James Bond films

MINOR 7ths – Jazz, Trance, Dance, Funk

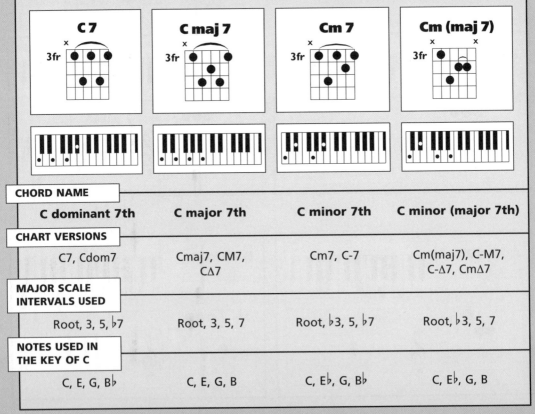

| CHORD NAME | | | |
|---|---|---|---|
| C dominant 7th | C major 7th | C minor 7th | C minor (major 7th) |
| **CHART VERSIONS** | | | |
| C7, Cdom7 | Cmaj7, CM7, CΔ7 | Cm7, C-7 | Cm(maj7), C-M7, C-Δ7, CmΔ7 |
| **MAJOR SCALE INTERVALS USED** | | | |
| Root, 3, 5, ♭7 | Root, 3, 5, 7 | Root, ♭3, 5, ♭7 | Root, ♭3, 5, 7 |
| **NOTES USED IN THE KEY OF C** | | | |
| C, E, G, B♭ | C, E, G, B | C, E♭, G, B♭ | C, E♭, G, B |

# Altered Triads

Sometimes we alter the basic major or minor chords to create a new chord that doesn't occur naturally as part of a scale or key. There are four types of altered triads.

## Augmented fifths

Augmented fifth chords (also called #5 chords or sometimes just augmented chords) raise the fifth of the triad by one semitone (in the case of C, this would raise the note of G to a G#). Common in jazz and some types of blues.

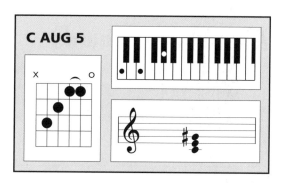

## Suspended fourths

Sus4s, as they're known, involve removing (or '**suspending**') the third of the chord and replacing it with the fourth note of the major scale. Appears in folk-rock. And church hymns.

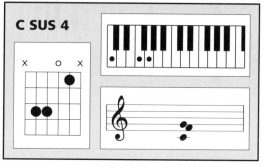

## Suspended seconds

Sus2s are created the same way – remove the third and replace it with the second note of the major scale. A favourite of hippy singer-songwriters and UK rock band **Skunk Anansie**.

## Diminished chords

If you flatten the third and fifth by a semitone each, you get a diminished chord. Most people play the four-part **diminished seventh** version by adding a double-flattened seventh on top too (in this case, a note of A, or B♭♭). Commonly used in jazz and classical music.

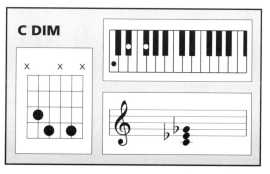

# Super-Octave Chords

If you go on adding notes higher than the octave to one of the types of seventh chords, you get these jazzy-sounding beasts. Just add odd-numbered intervals on top to create 9ths, 11ths and 13ths. Here are just a few examples of common super-octave chords.

## Altered Jazz chords

If you see a horrendous chord name like D7#5♭9/G it's not as scary as it looks. All the info you need about which notes to alter is in the chord name. D7#5♭9/G is actually a D7 chord (easy enough) but the fifth is raised a semitone (#5) and a flattened ninth has been added (♭9). The /G simply refers to the bass note – see opposite.

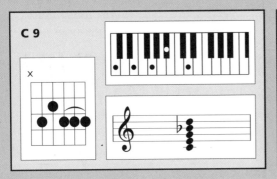

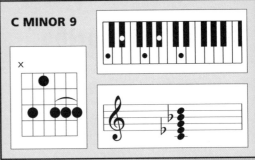

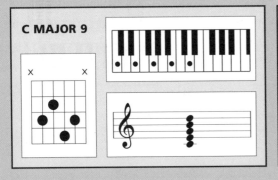

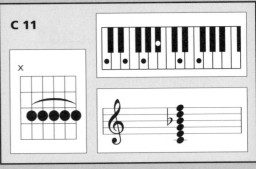

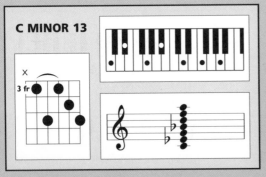

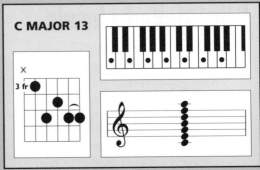

# Inversions And Slash Chords

We've touched on inversions already (it means that you play a chord with something other than its root note in the bass). Here, I've shown a chord of C major in root position (i.e. with the note of C in the bass) and in two inversions.

Inversions are notated on guitar chord charts using **slash notation** – the letter on the left of the slash is the chord name, and on the right is shown the bass note. Four-part chords can have three inversions, by putting the top note at the bottom - see the chord of C7/B♭ below.

**C (root position)**

**C/E (first inversion)**

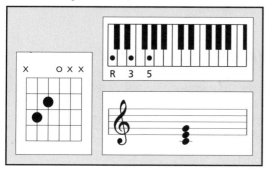
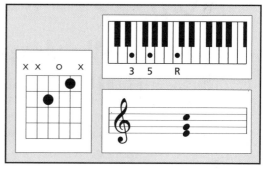

**C/G (second inversion)**

**C7/B♭ (third inversion)**

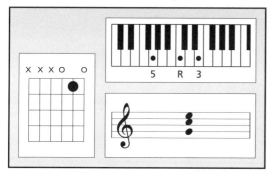
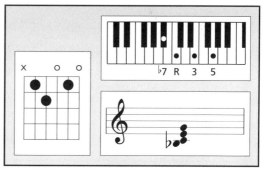

## More slash?

Sometimes, a chord is played with a completely different note in its bass – i.e. a note that doesn't normally appear as part of that chord at all. No problem – slash notation to the rescue! You can write *any* letter to the right of the slash. C/B is fine, as is D♭/G, or Cm7/A. This, again, is very common in jazz.

# Chord Charts – What Does It All Mean?

In the table below, you'll find all of the common chord types, together with the different ways you'll see them written in songbooks or charts.

Sorry that there isn't one simple system that everyone uses, but you know what musicians are like – they can never agree on anything, and anyway, it's great for starting arguments that can't be resolved one way or the other!

## Chord name conventions

Because of the different styles of guitarists throughout the world, several notation 'standards' have evolved. Below are several examples, all shown with a root note of C. On the left is printed the way you'll see chords in this book (usually the most common), followed by alternative namings.

| | |
|---|---|
| C | C major, Cmaj |
| Cm | Cmin, C- |
| C7 | Cdom7 |
| Cmaj7 | CM7, C△, C△7 |
| Cm7 | Cmin7, C-7 |
| C5 | C$^{(no\ 3rd)}$ |
| Caug | C+, C$^{+5}$ |
| C7$\sharp$9 | C7$^{(-10)}$, C7$^{(\flat10)}$ |

**Finally, if you don't know a chord, there's usually one that you do know which will fit just as well. Here are a few tips;**

• Chords ending in 9, 11 or 13 can usually be replaced with an equivalent 7th – e.g. if you don't know Cm11, Cm7 should be OK. If you can't play C9, try C7, and so on.
• In most cases, straight major or minor chords will work instead of 7ths or 9ths.
• Power chords (e.g. C5, A5 etc) can be used as a substitute for any major or minor chord, including 7ths, 9ths etc.

# Chord Progressions

Of course, all of this chord theory is pointless unless you are going to play more than one chord in a piece of music. When we string chords together like this it's referred to as a progression.

Progressions can be short (some dance music is based on a two-bar loop, for example) or longer (many jazz standards are 32 bars or more).

# When in Rome...

Sorry, but in music theory-land, chord progressions are referred to by Roman numerals. This is largely to differentiate between other uses of numbers (intervals, for example), but it can be a bit daunting to see all these Is and Vs all over the page. Here we go, then – I, II, III, IV, V, VI, VII. Now in French – un, deux, trois... er, maybe not.

# For example

So if, in rock terms, we talked about a chord sequence that went from C to F to G, we could call it a I–IV–V progression. This means that we're building a chord starting on the root, then the fourth, then the fifth of the home scale.

So why use the numbers? Because it makes it easier to **transpose**. If we want to play the same I-IV-V song in the key of G, we simply build triads on the root, fourth and fifth of the new key (so our progression would become G-C-D).

 # But what if...?

Sometimes, a progression might feature chords that seem to 'break the rules', like a major I chord followed by a major III chord (e.g. C to E chord change in a song). That's 'wrong' isn't it? Well, no, it's simply **non-diatonic**, meaning it uses harmony that is not purely based in one key. Every rule in music theory can be broken. If it sounds good.

# Chords Of The Major Scale

There are some chords that occur naturally just by choosing a note in the major scale and building a triad on it.

These are called **diatonic** chords (meaning 'in the key'). Just as with scales and modes, once you know the 'rules' of diatonic harmony, you can easily apply them to music in different keys.

## Diatonic chords in the key of C major

| C | Dm | Em | F | G | Am | B dim |
|---|----|----|---|---|----|---------|
| I | II | III | IV | V | VI | VII |
| major | minor | minor | major | major | minor | diminished |

Here, we can see that chord I in this major key is, unsurprisingly, major. Because of the way the tones and semitones naturally occur in the key, it so happens that chord II works out minor. Chord IV is major, and so on as you can see. But here's the good bit – *this stuff works in every single key!*

## Diatonic chords in the key of E major

| E | F#m | G#m | A | B | C#m | D#dim |
|---|-----|-----|---|---|-----|---------|
| I | II | III | IV | V | VI | VII |
| major | minor | minor | major | major | minor | diminished |

See what I mean? As long as you stay in key (i.e. keep to the key signature), chord III is *always* minor, and chord I is *always* major etc. Look at the chord suffixes – the major, minor and dim chords are the same for both keys.

# I, IV and V

We know that the three major chords that occur diatonically are those built on the root, fourth and fifth.

These are called **primary chords** in classical-speak. The simplest Country and Blues songs use these chords, as do children's nursery rhymes and some folk tunes. They're the most important chords in all music.

## Primary progression

**C major**

**G major**

**F major**

Here, I've shown three examples of a progression featuring I, IV and V chords, transposed into a different key each time. Note that the Roman numerals (i.e. the chords in the progression) stay the same, but the chords (i.e. the key) will change.

# II, III, VI and VII

There are four diatonically-occurring chords in the major scale which are not major.

Of these, three are minor (chords II, III and VI) and one is diminished (chord VII). Diminished chords are rare, so for these examples we're going to look at a **transposed progression** featuring diatonic major and minor chords.

# Major and minor progression

**C major**

| Am | G | F | Dm |
|----|---|---|----|
| VI | V | IV | II |

**G major**

| Em | D | C | Am |
|----|---|---|----|
| VI | V | IV | II |

**F major**

| Dm | C | B♭ | Gm |
|----|---|----|----|
| VI | V | IV | II |

Here, I've shown three examples of a progression featuring II, IV, V and VI chords, transposed into the same three keys as the previous example. Note that the chord types (i.e. major or minor) stay the same.

# Substitution

If you spend any time around jazzers
you'll hear them talk about 'substitution'.
It refers to the practice of playing one
chord instead of another to imply a third chord. So if, say, the chart suggests
a chord of Am (which contains notes of A, C and E) and the guitar plays C
(C, E and G), the implied chord (A,C, E and G) is Am7.

Obviously it's tricky to do this at speed, so in the table below I've supplied
some common examples of how it's achieved. All of these examples are chords
you might use if you were playing jazz in the key of A.

**Note** – this is advanced bluffing. Only to be attempted if you thoroughly
understand all the rest of the stuff about chords.

# Substitution table

| Original chord | Substitute with... | To create... |
|---|---|---|
| A, Amaj7 | C#m7 | Amaj9 |
| A7 | Em | A9 |
| Am, Am7 | Cmaj7 | Am9 |
| D, Dmaj7 | F#m7 | Dmaj9 |
| Dm | F | Dm7 |
| E7 | G#dim7 | E7(♭9) |

# Advanced substitutions

Sometimes, we play a substituted chord that by rights shouldn't work at all.
For example, if a jazzer saw A7 in a chart they might play an E♭7 over it. Sounds
bizarre?

Well, think about it. A7 contains A, C#, E and G. E♭7 contains E♭, G, B♭ and D♭.
Forget the G and D♭ for a moment (they appear in the chord of A7 anyway) and
you're left with only two notes which are different from the A7 chord – notes of
E♭ and B♭. So an A7 which uses E♭ and B♭ consists of the following notes – A, C#,
E♭, G, B♭. In other words, A7♭5♭9. Brain hurting yet?

**Django Reinhardt -** He may look cool, but his brain is calculating

# Aural Awareness or 'What, I'm supposed to listen, too?'

**Although this is near the back of the book, it's actually the most important section because it deals with the music we hear. A talented musician will always have an advanced level of aural skills, or a 'good ear', because it means they can understand what they're hearing and respond to it.**

Composers' aural skills have to be even better because they need to hear the music in their head before they write it (Beethoven famously continued to write music even when he was completely deaf).

Training your ear is very much like working out in the gym – you have to work on it regularly, and as time goes on, you gradually notice an improvement. However, there are a few tips which can make the process faster and less agonising than it might be.

# Aural workout

**Practise singing a melody and then try to play it back on your instrument.**

When you hear a song you like on the TV or radio, see if you can figure out the tune, or even the chords, without an instrument. Then check to see if you were right.

**Learn your intervals so you know them by sound as well as by note-names. Ask other musicians to play a chord and see if you can identify it.**

Listen to three- or four-part music (choirs, string quartets or rock harmonies) and see if you can sing the highest part (usually fairly easy) then the lowest (more difficult). If you're brave try to figure out the parts in between (very difficult indeed).

**When you're trying to figure out a progression, start by listening for the notes of the bass line. That will give you a starting point to work out what chords might be used.**

Try to develop a sense of 'relative pitch'. Play a note then sing a second above it, or a fifth above it or whatever, and then check on the instrument. Don't give up! Every bit of aural practice you do improves your skills.

# Recognising Chords

All chords have a particular flavour, and each has a different emotional impact on the listener. If you can feel this impact and remember how it feels, you'll start to recognise chords much faster.

This combination of 'feel' and memory is usually more effective – and quicker – than analysing every interval in a chord and trying to build it up theoretically. Don't worry if the 'feel' doesn't come straight away – everyone has this skill to a certain extent, and like all aural skills, it can be improved.

In the table below I've listed some common chords, with their theoretical construction, an example in C (so you can try them on a keyboard), and examples of how you might remember them by feel or musical style.

| Chord type | Construction | Example in C | Memory tips |
|---|---|---|---|
| Major | R, 3, 5 | C, E, G | Happy but bland-sounding. Uncomplicated. |
| Minor | R, ♭3, 5 | C, E♭, G | Darker or 'sadder' than a major chord but still simple-sounding. Common in rock music. |
| Dominant 7th | R, 3, 5, ♭7 | C, E, G, B♭ | Jazzy-sounding but still with a major-key feel. Used in rock, R&B, hymns. Sometimes feels unfinished, like it's got to resolve somewhere. |
| Minor 7th | R, ♭3, 5, ♭7 | C, E♭, G, B♭ | Even more Jazzy-sounding – darkly colourful. Feels very comfortable and warm – sounds 'sophisticated'. |
| Major 7th | R, 3, 5, 7 | C, E, G, B | Spacey, dreamy, floating major-feel chord. If used at the end of a progression, sounds particularly jazz-like; at the beginning often gives more of a Country feel. |
| Dominant 9th | R, 3, 5, ♭7, 9 | C, E, G, B♭, D | Complex and dark but still quite powerful-sounding. Funk and jazz spring to mind, but not rock and rarely classical. |
| Augmented 5th | R, 3, ♯5 | C, E, G♯ | Unfinished – if you don't play another chord after this you just *know* something bad will happen. |
| Diminished | R, ♭3, ♭5, (♭♭7) | C, E♭, G♭, A | Spooky! |

# Recognising Intervals

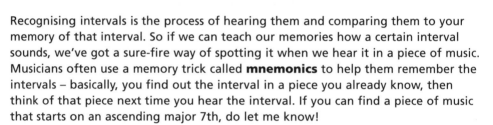

If you can recognise intervals by ear, it will improve every single aspect of your musicianship. You'll be able to **improvise** better (because you'll know what the notes sound like); your **sight reading** will be faster (because you'll instantly spot if you hit a wrong note); and you'll find it easier to work out **melodies** and **chord sequences** from recordings.

Recognising intervals is the process of hearing them and comparing them to your memory of that interval. So if we can teach our memories how a certain interval sounds, we've got a sure-fire way of spotting it when we hear it in a piece of music. Musicians often use a memory trick called **mnemonics** to help them remember the intervals – basically, you find out the interval in a piece you already know, then think of that piece next time you hear the interval. If you can find a piece of music that starts on an ascending major 7th, do let me know!

There are twelve intervals in the one-octave chromatic scale. These are listed in the table below – examples are given in the key of C. Next to each, I've given a mnemonic – i.e. a piece of music whose melody starts with those two ascending notes. Note – it doesn't matter how cheesy your mnemonics are, as long as you...

# Remember your intervals!

| | | |
|---|---|---|
| Minor second | **C-C♯** | Cello shark theme from *Jaws*. |
| Major second | **C-D** | First two notes of major scale, or of the *Eastenders* theme. |
| Minor third | **C-E♭** | First two notes of *Greensleeves*. |
| Major third | **C-E** | First two notes of 'While Shepherds Watched'. |
| Perfect fourth | **C-F** | 'Amazing Grace', or the two-note clean guitar riff from the verse of 'Smells Like Teen Spirit'. |
| Augmented fourth/ Diminished fifth | **C-F♯** | 'Maria' from *West Side Story*, or the main riff from 'Black Sabbath'. |
| Perfect fifth | **C-G** | Bugle call 'The Last Post'. |
| Minor sixth/ augmented fifth | **C-A♭** | (reversed) Theme from *Love Story*. |
| Major 6th | **C-A** | 'My Way'. |
| Minor 7th | **C-B♭** | 'Somewhere' from *West Side Story*. |
| Major 7th | **C-B** | None (but it's the strangest-sounding interval, so you should recognise it OK). |
| Perfect octave | **C-C** | Chorus of 'Somewhere Over The Rainbow'. |

# Recognising Progressions

If you combine your ability to spot intervals with your ability to recognise chords you'll be able to figure out whole progressions. But doing this at speed is not easy at first, so how do we go about developing this essential skill?

# The basics

All tonal music (i.e. music that uses chords and scales etc) has an implied pull to chord I i.e. the key, or **root**, chord. If you're playing away in the key of G major, any chord that you play which *isn't* G will feel less comfortable than any instances of the home chord of G. So the most important skill is to be able to 'feel' the I chord.

Try this: Play a chord of C, then Am, F and G (or G7). Notice that the progression doesn't sound complete until you play another chord of C. This is called a **resolution**. In Roman numeral terms, you've played a I, VI, IV, V, I progression.

In the table below I've shown some of the common simple chord changes (called **cadences** in classical-speak) that you'll hear in diatonic music. Their classical names are included for bluffing purposes but it's more important that you recognise them by sound and feel.

# Simple major key cadences

| Chord change | Example in the key of C | Feel | Classical name |
|---|---|---|---|
| V-I | **G major – C major** | Resolving, coming home | Perfect cadence |
| I-V | **C major – G major** | Hanging in the air, unfinished | Imperfect cadence |
| IV-I | **F major – C major** | Softly resolving – an 'Amen' chord change | Plagal cadence |
| V-VI | **G major – A minor** | Sounds like it's going to resolve, but doesn't | Interrupted cadence |

# Major or minor feel?

Tonal music always has a mainly major or minor feel to its key. You need to identify this early on because it will tell you where the home chord is, and help you to have a better idea what the other chords are likely to be. At any point in the track, stop the recording and ask yourself – if I had to play the ending NOW, would I play a minor chord or a major chord? Try both versions on an instrument if you're not sure. This will tell you the key.

# Improvising

**Surely, this is just making it up as you go along – so how can music theory be any use to us here? The answer is that when you're improvising over chord changes, you're not being completely 'free' at all – you're making theoretical choices about which notes will sound right over each chord. There are two main methods of improvising over changes – scalic and chord-tone.**

# Scalic improvising

With this system, you choose a scale (related to the key of the piece), and play it over the changes, using your ear to tell you if the notes sound right. As long as the chords are diatonic, the scale system works fine, although you'll find that some notes work better than others over any given chord.

# Chord-tone improvising

This is more difficult but much more effective than scale-based soloing alone. You need to know what the current chord is (from the chart) and what notes each chord contains (from your knowledge of chord construction), and then you choose single notes from the current chord to build a melody. With this system, you're guaranteed to play a solo that is free from wrong notes because every note 'works' with the current chord.

 # The Pentatonic wimp-out

This is a trick that all improvisers have resorted to at one time or another. If you're really stuck for what notes to play and can't follow the chords, simply choose any notes from the major or minor pentatonic scale (see page 66) depending on the feel of the piece. Because the pentatonic scale has only the most important notes in it, you're far less likely to hit a wrong one. It works. *If you can live with the shame.*

# Improv tips

- Don't always start a phrase on the first note of your scale – or the root note of the current chord.
- Use phrasing – once you've played a melody for three or four bars, leave a gap of a few beats.
- Use repetition – once you've made up a short melody that you like, play it again. Your solos will sound more melodic.

# Improvising — which scale to use?

On this page I've shown three chord progressions, each of which would need a different scale choice. And remember, if in doubt, pentatonic wimp-out!

# A major chord progression

**A major scale**

This progression is clearly in A major — we can tell by the key signature and the first chord. All the chords are diatonic (major I, major IV, minor II, major V). So the scale of A major would work a treat here.

# A minor chord progression

**A natural minor scale/ C major scale/ A minor pentatonic scale**

No sharps or flats in the key signature, so C major, right? No — this sequence is actually in A minor (note the first chord). Scale choices could include A natural minor, C major (you'd get away with it) or of course A minor pentatonic.

# 7th-based chord progression

**A minor pentatonic scale/ A major pentatonic scale**

Panic! A7, D7, E7 and some horrible jazz chord at the end. You could just about change scales rapidly for each chord, but your best bluffing bet here would have to be pentatonic unless you were prepared to think about chord tones (see the next page). A major pentatonic or A minor pentatonic would both work over these bluesy chords.

# Chord-Tone Improvising

If you know your **arpeggios**, this is the way to go. A chord tone (i.e. a note which is part of the current chord) will always 'work' musically, so you can add creativity with other elements such as tone, note length, dynamics and rhythm.

If you improvise with chord tones all the time it can all get a bit predictable and cheesy, but if your theory's up to it, it's a big improvement on randomly going up and down the same old scale shape (rock guitarists – *you know who you are!*)

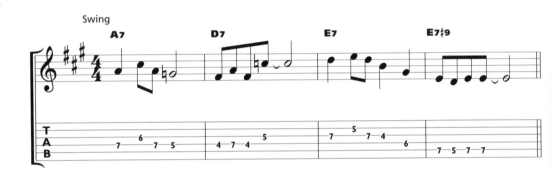

# Chord-tone improvising – solo analysis

**This melody uses notes of the current chord only. Let's look at a breakdown of why the player is choosing these particular notes.**

**Bar 1** uses a chord of A7 (notes of A, C#, E and G). The solo instrument plays notes of A, C#, A and G.

**Bar 2**'s D7 chord (D, F#, A and C) has the soloist playing F#, A, F# and C.

**Bar 3** is an E7 arpeggio (E, G#, B and D) so the melody uses notes of D, E, D, B and G#.

In **bar 4**, the player panics. "E7#9 – I can't think fast enough" (it actually uses notes of E, G#, B, D and G). Because they know that there's a basic E7 chord there, they get away with playing just two notes – E and D. And the audience is none the wiser. Outrageous bluffing!

# Advanced Improvising

In this example, the solo is based on arpeggio notes, but also uses **passing notes** (i.e. notes which are part of the home key but are adjacent to the notes of the current chord) and also **chromatic passing notes** (notes which are not part of the scale but are a semitone above or below a chord tone).

All passing notes have to resolve somewhere – usually to a chord tone. A truly great jazz solo could make use of **scales**, **chord tones**, **passing notes** and **chromatics**. And if someone says you're soloing off key you can always say you were 'pushing the chromaticism'. Yeah, right...

\* = Chromatic note
P = Passing note

# Advanced improvising – solo analysis

**Here, all of the notes are chord tones except those marked with a P (passing notes) and a \* (chromatic passing notes). Let's look in detail at what's going on.**

In **bar 1** (A7), the soloist starts on a chord tone of A, then plays a 'wrong' note of C. But hold on – it's a chromatic passing note, resolving to the chord tone of C♯. The other notes in the bar are all chord tones, except the last note of D♯, which is leading to...

...**bar 2**, where along with the D7 chord tones our soloist plays a chromatic passing note of G♯ (resolving to A), and a regular passing note of B.

In **bar 3**, the E7 chord sees a chromatic passing note of G, resolving to the chord tone of G♯...

...and this time in **bar 4** our player doesn't panic during that E7♯9. A triplet lick of passing and chromatic notes resolves to E7 chord tones all the way with one quick chromatic A♯ before the fourth beat of the bar.

# Outro

You will have discovered that there are two types of musician – Rock people and Classical people. They play different instruments, have different training and speak a completely different theoretical language.

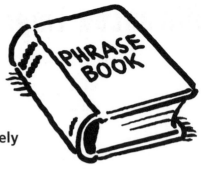

In this book I've attempted to give you as much of an impartial view of music theory as possible, but whichever side you come from, sometimes you'll need to translate the jargon from the people on the Other Side. Here, I've included some of the expressions that musicians use, and given both versions of them. **Keep this guide with you at all times. Now get out there and start bluffing!**

# Musicians translated

| Classical-speak | Rock-speak |
|---|---|
| Aeolian mode | Natural minor scale |
| Cadences | Changes |
| Cadenza | Solo |
| Coda | Outro |
| Concert | Gig |
| Crotchets | 4s |
| Down beat | The 'one' |
| Ensemble | Band |
| Exposition | Start |
| Forte | Loud |
| Fortissimo | Very loud |
| Glissando | Slide |
| Minims | 2s |
| Modulation | Key change |
| Motif | Lick |
| Ostinato | Riff |
| Pianissimo | What? |
| Piano | Soft |
| Polyrhythm | Groove |
| Programme | Set list |
| Quavers | 8s |
| Score | Chart |
| Semiquavers | 16s |
| Trumpet mute | Wah-wah pedal |
| Tutti | Full band |

# Musician jokes

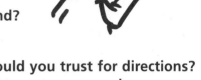

**What's the difference between
an oboe and an onion?**
Nobody cries when you chop up an oboe.

**What's the definition of a minor second?**
Two flautists playing in unison.

**If you were lost in the woods who would you trust for directions?
An in-tune tenor sax player, an out-of-tune tenor sax player or
Santa Claus?**
The out-of tune tenor sax player. The other two are hallucinations.

**How do you make a chain saw sound like a baritone sax?**
Add vibrato.

**What's the range of a tuba?**
Twenty yards if you've got a good arm.

**How many drummers does
it take to change a light bulb?**
None (they have machines to do that now.)

**How can you tell if a violin is out of tune?**
The bow is moving.

**Why did the chicken cross the road?**
To get away from the bassoon recital.

**How do you make a violin sound like a viola?**
Sit in the back and don't play.

**What's the difference between a soprano and the IRA?**
You can negotiate with the IRA.

**Why are violins smaller than violas?**
They're really the same size. Violinists' heads are larger.

**Why do bagpipers walk when they play?**
To get away from the noise.

**How do you get a guitar player to play softer?**
Give him a sheet of music.

# Index

# The players

# Musical terms

If you've enjoyed this book, why not check out the other books in this great new series, available from all good music and book retailers, or in case of difficulty, direct from Music Sales (see page 2).

# It's Easy To Bluff...

| Blues Guitar | Rock Guitar | Metal Guitar | Acoustic Guitar | Jazz Guitar |
|---|---|---|---|---|
| AM955196 | AM955218 | AM955207 | AM955174 | AM955185 |

**JOE BENNETT** has been teaching guitar for fifteen years, and regularly works as a session guitarist. He is also a senior examiner in electric guitar for The London College of Music and Head of Popular Music at City of Bath College. Joe's publications include the *Guitar: To Go!* and *Really Easy Guitar* series, and *The Little Book of Scales*, plus tracks and articles for *Future Music*, *PowerOn* and *Total Guitar* magazines.

www.musicsales.com